D1711990

To My Second Momma!

I have loved you since I met you at 14 years old. I thank you for being my "invisible" best friend through it all! God Bless You & much

Love, your daughter,
Aurelia Ripon

July 16th 2014
#143 of first 200

Deborah Aubrey-Ripon,
author

Books by Deborah Aubrey-Peyron

Miraculous Interventions™
True life stories of miraculous events
that have shaped the author's life
and those she has known.

Christmas Chaos!
A family with three unruly boys have a
less-than-fortunate run-in with St. Nicholas!
An illustrated children's Christmas story
told with humor, verse,
and Christ, of course!

Miraculous Interventions™ II
Modern Day Priests, Prophets, Pastors
And Everyday Visionaries
Amazing stories from various ministers who walk
in the office of the miraculous.
These are their experiences with the Lord
and the divine interventions they have witnessed.

Miraculous Interventions™ III
2012 - The Miraculous Year
Due for release late winter 2013

Miraculous Interventions™ II
Modern Day Priests, Prophets, Pastors & Everyday Visionaries

*Amazing Stories from Various
Pastors, Lay Ministers and
Those Who are Called to Walk
In the Office of the Miraculous*

*Their Experiences with the Lord
And the Divine Interventions They
Have Witnessed*

By
Deborah Aubrey-Peyron

Home Crafted Artistry & Printing
New Albany, IN 47150
2012

This publication is intended to provide accurate and authoritative information in regard to the subject matter covered. The statements and opinions expressed in this book are those of the author and the pastors whose works are recorded here. All scripture quotations in this book are taken from the King James Version of the Bible unless otherwise noted. All stories presented in this book have been told with the expressed permission of the persons involved as much as possible. Where it has not been possible or was requested, the names and places have been changed.

Copyright 2012 by Deborah Aubrey-Peyron. All rights reserved.
Published by Home Crafted Artistry & Printing 2012 with permission.

Proudly printed in the United States of America.

Except for brief quotations and except as permitted under the United States Copyright Act of 1976, no part of this publication may be reproduced or distributed in any form or means without written permission of the publisher or author.

ISBN 13: 978-0-9827621-9-6
ISBN 10: 0 98276 219 4

Home Crafted Artistry & Printing
Mary Dow Smith, Chief Editor
1252 Beechwood Avenue
New Albany, IN 47150
Contact information:
e-mail HomeCraftedArtistry@yahoo.com
e-mail peyronsinjesus@yahoo.com

Special Orders
Special discounts are available on quantity purchases of 25 or more copies.
Speaking or signing engagements may be arranged upon request.
Please e-mail or write to the above address.

"*Miraculous Interventions*" is a trademark of Deborah Aubrey-Peyron and is reserved exclusively for this series of books.
Walt Disney World is a registered trademark of WDW, Orlando FL and is not an endorser of this publication. WDW is not affiliated with Home Crafted Artistry and Printing nor with Deborah Aubrey-Peyron, author of Miraculous Interventions.

Cover design by Mary Dow Bibb Smith
Photographs are author's photographs.
Scripture on cover quoted from
Matthew 10:27 NIV
Jeremiah 33:3 KJ

DEDICATION

For all the pastors named here *[in alphabetical order]*
and all their good works of mercy,
Peace be with you:

Ministers Jim and Ann Carter
Lay ministers Larry and Marilynn Crosier
Evangelist and ordained minister Rev. Ivie Dennis
Anglican Priest, Fr. Michael Olsen and wife, Patricia
Retired Methodist Pastor Leland Schwarz,
and his wife Anne
Father Bernie Weber, Religious Order of the
Passionist Priests, pastor and missionary
and all the Everyday Ministers that reach out
and touch people's lives
one person at a time.

Grace and peace be unto you all.

And for you, dear readers,
this book is dedicated for you.

*"Beloved, I wish above all things
that thou mayest prosper
and be in health,
even as thy soul prospereth."*
3 John 2

Love and blessings,

Deb

TABLE OF CONTENTS

Acknowledgements . . . 13

Introduction 15

SECTION ONE: "Divine Set Ups" . 19

Fr. Bernie Weber:

*Religious Order of the Passionist Priests,
Pastor and Missionary*

My Introduction to Fr. Bernie . . . 20

Incredible Journeys 22

A Divine Set Up 23

Brother Bernie. 24

The Faith of a Blind Woman . . . 26

Sylvia's Stories   Part One . . 28

                        Part Two . . 30

The Healing of Two Hearts . . . 31

First Day on the Job . . . 32

Fill My Church 33

Healing the Blind 35

A Woman's Retreat 36

A Priest's Retreat 40

Medjugorje 42

Deliver Us from Evil 45

Level Five 47

A Perfect Job 49

A Normal Heart 50

I'm Free!! 52

Come Back! 53

Spirit of Epilepsy 55

Yes, Jesus Loves Me! 56

Short Stories, One, Two and Three . . 57

SECTION TWO: "Used by God Unawares" 59
Leland and Anne Schwarz
    Retired Methodist Minister and His Wife

The Singapore Incident . . . 60
A Little One 61
In the Beginning...Lee 62
Holy Spirit Come! 63
In the Beginning...Anne . . . 65
The Meeting of Two Hearts . . . 67
Unbinding the Gospel 69
My Introduction to the Schwarz's
        "Saint Anne" 72
Second Day of Class 73
A Closely Guarded Secret . . . 75
A Christmas Miracle 76
The Road to Seattle – or The Search for God's
    Sense of Humor 81
        Resort 84
        Boots in the Wall . . . 87
        Columbia River Gorge . . 89
        At Last! 91
The Hand of God 97
Another Little One 100
The Thrill of His Presence . . . 101
Read the Book! 102
A Week of Dreams for Lee . . . 103
Discovering Your Call . . . 105

SECTION THREE: "Street Minister, Hell Shrinker

.   107

Pastor Ivie Dennis
Evangelist

How She Came to Serve God   .   .   110
Mission Trip, 1500 Souls   .   .   114
On the Third Day the Lame Walked   .   .   115
Resurrection of the Dead – The 4th Day   .   116
The Great Feast   117
Stepping Out in Faith   118
Our Introduction to Rev. Ivie Dennis   .   119
Meeting the Peyrons – In Her Own Words   .   121
Building by the Brook   .   .   .   122
The Little Yellow House   .   .   .   123
Breaking of the Bread   .   .   .   124
Feeding Angels Unawares   .   .   .   126
Shoe Boxes   127
Close Encounters of the Godly Kind   .   .   128
Momma Eddie   131
Hospice   134
A Dog's Tale Introduction   .   .   .   135
A Dog's Tale by Rev. Ivie Dennis   .   .   137
The Road to Home   142

SECTION   FOUR: "Lay Ministers for the Lord"

.   .   145

Pastor Jim and Ann Carter
Minister and His Wife

Precious Gifts   146
The First Supper   148
Rough Starts   149

Jim's Story 150
Notre Dame 153
More of Jim's Story 154
Ann's Story 155
Sound Doctrine 156
The Trouble with Religion . . . 157
Believing Above All Else . . . 158
Jim's Prophesy 159
Jim's Word of Knowledge for Me . . 160
Ann's Prophesy for Me . . . 160
Jim and Ann Carter, Ministers Address . 161

SECTION FIVE: "Praying for a Florida Cracker"
. . 163

Larry and Marilynn Crosier
Lay Ministers for Christ

A Florida Cracker 165
Home Sweet Home 166
Spiritual Warfare 167
Season of Healing 168
A Double Portion 169
The River of Life 170
Intercessor 171
Orders Luke 4: 18-19 . . . 172
Move 173
A Dream Come True 174
A Glimpse of What Is to Come . . 175
Looking for the Pine Tree . . . 176
Looking for Land 177
Dry Spell 178
Show Me the Next Step – More Prophesy . 179

SECTION SIX: "St Columba of Iona
Community Church".   .   .   .   181

Father Michael Olsen and Patricia Olsen
    Anglican Priest and Pastor, and His Wife

Coincidence on Top of Coincidence .   .   182
Help A Brother Out   184
January 1, 2012 – Introduction   .   .   186
Signs and Wonders   188
Confirmation   195

SECTION SEVEN: *"The Rest of Us!"*   .   197
Everyday Ministers and Visionaries

Chris Luken – Youth Minister,
        Church of the Epiphany   .   .   198
Mary and Mitch Smith –
        A Miracle Over the Wire   .   .   200
George Stoddard – Second Chance .   .   201
Frances Gregory –
        A Diamond In a Cookie Box .   .   204
Jean Crook - An Afternoon with Miss Jean .   208
        A Long Time Coming.   .   .   212
Mitchell Smith – The Mending of Mitch   .   216
        St. Joseph   217
        Daddy   218
        Second Chances   .   .   .   220
        Mitch's Testimony: As Real as Rocks!   221

SECTION EIGHT: Emissary of Yeshua the Messiah

.   .   223

Deborah Aubrey-Peyron
   Evangelist and Author

Adversary - Part One   224
The Best Made Plans of Mice and Men Don't
   Compare to the Best Made Plans of God .   228
St. Teresa of Calcutta: Part One   .   .   232
                        Part Two   .   .   235
                        Part Three   .   .   236
                        Part Four   .   .   237
An Interesting Week in the Spring   .   .   238
Adversary - Part Two   240
The Key   241
A Cry Out   242
Happy Father's Day   244
Do Not Fear!   245
No Miracle Today   247
A Gold Car   251
Healed and Whole   253
Saved Once Again   255
The Christmas Story Lady – All God's Plan
   The Making of "*Christmas Chaos!*"   .   257
Our First Christmas Chaos!   .   .   .   265
The Last Story of 2011   .   .   .   267

ACKNOWLEDGMENTS

As before, I thank my God, and savior, Jesus Christ for being the author and finisher of my faith (Hebrews 12:2), and any books I have written.

I thank my family and friends who always support and help me in all my endeavors. I breathe a little easier with you around.

For this book, I thank the pastors and lay ministers who have so boldly told their stories for the glory of God. I praise God for all of you in my life.

I also thank my lay minister friends who go about quietly doing God's miracles here on earth. Thanks for allowing me to "blow your cover".

I thank Karen Jensen who signed on to help with all the technical end of the writing. Your patience with me and your joyful attitude were an absolute blessing!

Gracious thanks to Lisa Boneck for doing a final proof-reading on extremely short notice. You're the best!

And to my dear Mary, we are friends and now co-workers. Thank you for being my publisher, chief editor, and cover designer. Where did you get more than 24 hours in your days?

God Bless you one and all.

INTRODUCTION

Many people in their lifetime, if they know one true miracle worker besides Jesus Christ, they consider themselves very blessed. What are the odds of one person being close friends with many true miracle workers scattered everywhere from Seattle, Washington to Orlando, Florida?

That is an interesting question. Maybe it was because our spirits recognized each other's spirit and in that way we became close. We just drug our flesh along with us for the ride. I am not talking about "celebrity" pastors on the television (nothing against television Evangelists). I am talking about everyday visionaries. These people, whom I have had the privilege of calling friends, are out on the streets or in small home churches calling people to God the Father, Jesus Christ and the Holy Spirit.

They have called people utilizing God's miracles, signs and wonders and with visions and gifts of the Holy Spirit. He is calling all to Christ no matter where they sit in a pew on a Saturday or a Sunday.

Having sat and listened to them tell their stories and written them down has been a wonderful treat for me. Not only have they fascinating stories to tell, but how they were called by God are stories in themselves. Even how I met each individual is another fine narrative.

For me, this is a more enjoyable book to have written than my first one. Not necessarily easier, just not so much about me. These were whole new adventures to go on just by turning the page. How exciting! Let's get started. My hope is that you enjoy our journey too!

Welcome to "Miraculous Interventions II".

Shalom,
Deborah Aubrey-Peyron, Author

"*The Lord* shall establish thee
an holy people unto Himself,
as He hath sworn unto thee,
if thou shalt keep the commandments
of the Lord thy God,
and walk in His ways."
Deuteronomy 28:9

"And as ye go, preach, saying,
the kingdom of heaven is at hand.
Heal the sick, cleanse the lepers,
raise the dead, cast out devils:
freely ye have received,
freely give."
Matthew 10: 7,8

"Behold, I will send my messenger,
and he shall prepare the way before me..."
Malachi 3:1

"If you don't see miracles,
just adjust your vision"
Deb Peyron

SECTION ONE
FATHER BERNIE WEBER

"DIVINE SET UPS"

Born September 7th, 1942
Joined Passionist Order, September 1974
Born in the Holy Spirit December 7, 1973
He walks in the Holy Spirit filled gifts of Speaking in
Tongues, Healing, and Words of Knowledge.
His Mission Field is to bring the Holy Spirit to Catholic
Parishioners.

Father Bernie lives on donations by making candles, blessing them for a healing ministry, and selling them at his Holy Spirit Seminars. This is how he makes gas money to get from place to place since he has taken a vow of poverty.

Father Bernie was specifically given orders from God to be in healing ministry, reconciliation, and intercessory prayer. He was ordained as a priest, then a pastor. He has seen one vision in his life, so far, and has witnessed many miraculous instances over the 36+ years he has been in ministry.

I think if he were to tell every miracle he has ever seen, it would take another 36 years to write them all down.

Father Bernie asked me to change all the names of the cities, churches and people for their own privacy. I have respected his wishes and done so. I stayed as close to the actual words and emotions Bernie used in his stories as I could reasonably do.

Thanks for understanding
– the Author

Fr. Bernie Weber with me at the Passionist convent during our interview.

As his stories unfolded we were swept away to other times and places.

MY INTRODUCTION TO
FATHER BERNIE WEBER

My interest in Fr. Bernie began over three and a half years ago. A lady in our prayer meeting had come by to say that there was to be a Holy Spirit Seminar going on at St. Joe's and suggested that some of the people in our group might care to attend. She went on to talk a little about the priest in charge, Fr. Bernie Weber. He was known for dealing in the miraculous. It caught my interest right away. A Holy Spirit Seminar! Maybe this man could explain some of the things I had witnessed and experienced in my life. Finally, answers! This was something for me and still is.

I showed up at the second meeting they had with a pen and a pad of paper. Each meeting was at least two hours long once a week for a month. I committed to the time and went without my husband. He taught from a book called "Following the Holy Spirit", the Holy Bible, and called on many personal stories of his own.

He told his stories with humor and real emotions. From laughter to tears, we all walked with him through one miracle story after another. He introduced me to two very fine ladies, Debbie and Judy whom I now call friends. They are fine examples of powerful praying women.

Father Bernie said you can only receive miracles with an open heart. You have to have complete faith. He categorizes them in five levels.

1) LEVEL ONE: Minor Healings, such as bad knees, headaches, skin rashes, minor illness, relational healings, etc.

2) LEVEL TWO: Healing faster than in normal circumstances. Such as broken bones, cancers, etc.

3) LEVEL THREE: Minor Miracles– People coming off crutches and walkers right away.

4) LEVEL FOUR: Absolute Incredible Healings–in front of your eyes; instantly healed from various illnesses such as cancer, broken bones, high temperatures, etc.

5) LEVEL FIVE: Instantaneous Regeneration– impossible to explain by man, such as: blind seeing, deaf hearing, terminal cancer disappearing, and once a doctor-pronounced dead woman coming back to life with no human intervention except prayer.

INCREDIBLE   JOURNEYS

Some incredible journeys start in the most comfortable of places. My husband, Mark, accompanied me one early afternoon on a warm spring day to a monastery in Louisville, Kentucky to interview Fr. Bernie for the new book I was starting on Miraculous Pastors.

We arrived on time at a large brick building where Father warmly greeted us at the door. I brought an hour and a half tape and a pad of paper thinking we would be there that amount of time. I thought I was prepared. Surely I did not know the man as well as I thought.

He settled us down into a small meeting room. There were several chairs and a couple of end tables scattered throughout the room. I set the tape recorder on the table next to me and Father Bernie sat across from me. Mark was across the room from us taking pictures for the new book.

I asked some basic background questions and took notes. After getting all the preliminary data of his birth, education and how he got involved in his ministry, I asked him to start telling miracle stories. Then Father Bernie Weber started telling miraculous stories as fast as he could. It went something like this . . .

A DIVINE SET UP

When I listened to Father Bernie tell his story, it seemed he almost didn't make it to the seminary. When Bernie came home for Christmas from Hawaii his father prophesied that he would one day become a priest. But Bernie wanted to teach, and he was a good high school math teacher. He also thought about getting married some day. He would have to give all that up, too. So he started to pray. And pray. And at the age of 32, God called him to the Passionist Order.

Bernie was already hearing God speak to him, giving him words of knowledge and seeing miracles even before the very beginning of his seminary days. One would have thought he would be happily saying yes to God constantly.

Did I mention Father Bernie's slight stubborn streak and at times a possibly less than grateful attitude towards speaking words of knowledge to people that he didn't particularly want to talk to at all in the first place?

"You want me to do what, Lord?!"
"Tell them what? I'm not sure I want to talk to her/him at all! Loorrdd!!"

But in the end, the answer was always the same,
"Okay, Lord. It must be one of your Divine set ups."

BROTHER   BERNIE

While he was "Brother" Bernie, he was assigned to make rounds at the local Catholic Hospital. One day, Bernie was visiting an Italian lady from his church.

He walked into her hospital room. She was lying in the bed with her sheets pulled up to her neck. She was not feeling very well. As they talked, she told Brother Bernie about her daughter in the Intensive Care Unit right above her floor. She went on to say, "If God wants one of us, take me. I'm ready. Spare my daughter."

Brother Bernie replied, "Mrs. Marconi, God doesn't have to take either one of you." Her roommate was a German woman. He could feel the coldness emanating from her. This woman would sit and scowl at them while they talked. When Brother Bernie was ready to leave he made the mistake of thinking, "Thank God I don't have to talk to her." He left without saying a word to her.

He came back on Saturday to visit again. The Italian lady's bed was empty.

But Miss Ice Box, was sitting right there in her chair. Bernie was taken by surprise. He asked, "What happened to Mrs. Marconi?" The German woman answered him curtly, "She went home."

"Oh."

Brother Bernie thought to himself, "Well, no reason for me to stay here, I'm leaving." God stopped him dead in his tracks.

"TALK TO THE GERMAN WOMAN."

"I don't want to."

There was silence.

Sigh.

 "Okay."

And out of Brother Bernie's mouth came, "Well, since

Mrs. Marconi is gone and you are still here, mind if I talk to you?"

Gruffly, "No, go ahead."

Brother Bernie went around and sat on her bed. He didn't know what else to say. Then she broke down. A general confession came out of her mouth. She hadn't been to confession in over 45 years. She drove her husband to the grave, she alienated all her children. She had no friends. She had been mean! Real mean!

Everything came out! It came pouring out! He just sat there listening, not knowing what to say. When she finally got through, he looked at her and said, "All your life you have controlled others. You are angry because you can't control God. Do you want Jesus to come into your heart and forgive you?"

"Yes." She prayed with Brother Bernie. The coldness was gone. She promised to go to confession when she got out of the hospital, but God had other plans. She died that very night. In Bernie's eyes, she had already been forgiven.

THE FAITH OF A BLIND WOMAN

In 1978, again while he was still "Brother" Bernie, he was assigned to a hospital way up in the northern states. One evening, he went in a certain room and saw a blind woman visiting a man dying of emphysema. She was Catholic, and her spirit was so beautiful that he felt she was visiting him! He was very touched by her faith. After a while, she left.

The man was in an oxygen tent with his family sitting nearby. He was not Catholic, but he said to Brother Bernie, "I wish I had the faith of that blind woman." Then Brother Bernie asked him if he wanted to say an act of contrition. He was a Protestant, but he still said. "Yes!" So they prayed.

He went into a coma later that Wednesday night.

By Friday night when Bernie was on night duty, he went in to pray with him again while he was still in a coma. Brother Bernie sang songs to him for a half an hour, from 9:30 until 10 pm.

At 10 pm the man's wife and son came in and stood at the foot of the bed. All three of them stood there. The wife pulled out a rosary.

"Do you want to say a rosary?"

"Yes."

They said the Apostle's Creed and got to the first decade and said, "Blessed Mother take him."

At the Second decade, it was the same. "Blessed Mother, take him."

At the Third decade, half way through, the old gentleman stopped breathing. They all stopped speaking. Then all three of them felt peace fall over them. All sound disappeared. Time stood still. Then, after a few seconds they could hear and move again. Yes, indeed, Mary had come for him.

The wife stayed with her husband for another 20

minutes. The son and Brother Bernie left the room and let her have her time to say good-bye. Then he got to hear their story.

She was Catholic and her husband was a Lutheran. He worked hard, smoked hard and swore hard. Then he got emphysema. He was on a one way street down hill. She started praying the rosary every day that he would not die until he turned to Christ. She knew when she came in the room that night that he was still lost.

But as he was dying, Mary came to tell him, Christ heard his prayer. He was forgiven.

You see, he truly did have the faith of the blind woman after all.

SYLVIA'S STORIES

STORY NUMBER ONE

Bernie's very first prayer meeting was held in an apartment near the ghetto in a big metropolitan city. He was in the beginning of his second year of theology. There were people from the neighborhood attending. Brother Bernie was the only Caucasian in the room. The theme song the group always opened with was, "Yahweh, I Know You are Near." There was a quick half hour of prayer, and it was very simple. Then they went in the kitchen for some fruit punch and fellowship.

Even though Brother Bernie was scared to lead his very first prayer meeting by himself, he got through it. It all went well, and people came back!

By the second meeting there was one white woman from the projects who had been invited. Her name was Sylvia. The group again had their half hour prayer meeting. When the meeting was over, some of the ladies started getting up to go to the kitchen and help with the fruit punch. All of a sudden, Sylvia burst forth crying and she started "spilling her guts" to Brother Bernie. She kept saying how sorry she was. The poor lady was crying incredibly hard. No one knew what was happening. People were going bananas!

Bernie went running up to her and automatically started praying for her. One Pentecostal sister started playing the piano and praising God. To hear him tell it, it was chaos! He didn't know what to do! Finally Sylvia settled down. She started to tell her story.

Sylvia said when they started the prayer meeting she was looking at Brother Bernie. His attire was casual. She was sitting opposite him in a chair. While she was looking at him, all of a sudden everything disappeared but his face. She

28

said a golden glow appeared around his face. Then his face turned to the face of Jesus!

For the whole half hour they were praying, Sylvia sat transfixed looking at the face of Jesus! And Jesus was looking back at her! That was why at the end of the prayer meeting she started to cry so hard! She couldn't take it anymore. Even though she was raised Catholic, she had been away from the church for over 45 years.

At one time in her life, Sylvia had lived in a Park Avenue Penthouse. She had jewels, furs, money, but no God. But now, she lived in the inner city, married to an alcoholic with two children. She was on welfare in a dead end life. She felt no possibility of anything good in her life. Sylvia's ankle's hurt her so badly that she could hardly walk. There was no way that she could get a job. She was alienated from God. She had no friends. She felt she had no hope in her life.

Then she came to the prayer meeting and saw Jesus!

There Brother Bernie was, brand new at holding prayer meetings, sitting in the parlor not completely knowing what to do for her and God stepped right out of time then and there and healed her heart. She had a conversion and her life began to change. Her health healed, she looked for a job and became the most faithful person attending church that he had!

SYLVIA'S STORIES

STORY NUMBER TWO

Some time after her conversion Sylvia's husband went on a drinking binge. She had two children that her husband couldn't have cared less about. Sometimes the children would come to the meetings, but the husband chose alcohol over Jesus every time.

While she was still on welfare, she had saved $40.00 out of her check. So, she went to the store with this money and bought groceries. There was no more money for the rest of the month. The groceries had to last until the next check arrived. Sylvia got home with her groceries, and she found two twenty dollar bills in the bottom of the sack. She went back up to the store the next day and saw the manager. She told him, "I found these two twenty dollar bills in the bottom of my sack." He told her, "We weren't short yesterday, keep them." Wow. She now had $40.00 more for groceries.

She ended up getting a job as a cashier at that same grocery store because she had shown herself to be honest.

Father Bernie likens this story to the widow woman with Elijah. Oil and grain that would have been just enough for one meal for her and her son instead lasted to feed the three of them a year and a half!

THE HEALING OF TWO HEARTS

When Brother Bernie worked in the inner city, it was during his second year of theology when they used to hold a little prayer meeting in a neighborhood woman, Pam's house. Brother Bernie was scared to death because he rode his bicycle there through the ghetto. Or, even if he rode the bus it was still a six block walk from the bus stop to the heart of the ghetto where she lived. He was always in prayer. The whole year there, riding or walking back and forth, he was never touched or bothered.

Pam told Br. Bernie of a family that lived a couple of houses away, Laverne and her daughter. Laverne had a mentally retarded daughter who was in her 40's. This mother absolutely hated her daughter. Pam told the story that once long ago, in the middle of winter, Laverne had thrown her daughter outside in her nightgown. The men in the neighborhood took terrible advantage of her in the way that some men will.

One night Pam asked Brother Bernie to go with her to pray for the daughter, the one that had been abused. (Laverne's daughter had the mental age of a five year old.) As Br. Bernie and Pam moved to pray for the girl, Bernie invited her mother to come and pray for her as well. When Laverne approached her daughter, the daughter raised her hands over her head to protect herself. After all, her mother was always beating on her. Bernie said to the girl, "No, mother isn't going to hurt you. We are going to pray for you."

Hands were held and prayer began. When they started praying, the mother started crying. Then the daughter started crying. When they embraced each other everyone started crying! Only God can heal hearts in an instant.

Wow!

FIRST DAY ON THE JOB

By the time Father Bernie had been ordained a pastor and received his first parish, he had been in the ministry business quite a while. Still, nothing he had been through had prepared him for his first day on the job.

His mission from his Provincial was to take this small parish and build it from scratch. But God's mission started him on a different foot entirely.

Father Bernie went into his office early that morning only to be met with three crises on hand! Someone brought in their daughter with possible lupus. He immediately prayed for her and later there were no signs of lupus. A lady in her 80's came by who had severe arthritis in both hands. Father Bernie again prayed for her and she was instantly healed! She was so excited that she immediately thought of her brother, Floyd, who was in his 60's and in the hospital. He could surely use a miracle as well!

So off he went to see Floyd in the hospital. When he arrived at his room, Floyd's brother was there and he related this story to Father Bernie: Three days before Father saw Floyd, he had had surgery for terminal cancer. All the doctors could do was to sew him back up. Could Father Bernie please help him?

Father Bernie walked over to Floyd's bed side, laid hands on the man and prayed for him. The elderly man started crying. He felt something go through him. Two days later, this man was again in pain due to a bowel obstruction. The surgeon once again opened him up. The surgeon removed the obstruction and looked for the terminal cancer and it was gone! Then, while Floyd was in the hospital recuperating from surgery, his daughter won a car! He went home with a newly healed body in his daughter's brand new car!

FILL MY CHURCH

It was a cold night in January of 1983 at a local parish. Father Bernie was at a devotion to the Blessed Mother. He had started this public healing service once a month on Saturday nights. They prayed the rosary, then there was adoration of the Blessed Sacrament, a litany, the reading of scripture in the holy name of Jesus, there was the laying on of hands for the sick, preaching, blessing with the monstrance and closing.

He held these services until May of that year. The attendance unfortunately was poor. While on a trip to southern California, Father Bernie consulted with the Lord on what to do. God said, "NEVER QUIT OUT OF DISCOURAGEMENT."

At the May meeting several things happened. During the praying of the Rosary a lady there with a degenerated hip socket, suddenly felt as though her hip joint was on fire on the inside. The hip pain subsided and never bothered her for the rest of her earthly life!

There was also another lady, Leslie, there that night who regularly attended his meetings and was clairaudient*. She told Father Bernie, "The Lord spoke to me and He wanted me to give you a message: you are doing a good job. Keep up the good work. Then the Blessed Mother said, 'You have tried to fill this church and have failed. Now I will fill it in honor of My Son.'"

Father Bernie kept these messages a secret from December of 1983 to December of 1984. This was a special holy year declared from Pope John Paul II. He called it in honor of Mary.

*"Clairaudient" [French]: to clearly hear a spoken word from God. They are called locutions.

Almost a year had gone by. It was September. He had had ten months to fill the church and Father Bernie hadn't even come close. While he was praying for the healing of a woman's ankle, he went into a vision. In an instant, he saw the whole church full of people. Then he was given the gift of locutions. The Blessed Mother spoke to Father Bernie. *[He did not tell me what she told him]*

The next month of October he saw this vision come true. The church was full! A Baptist woman dying with bone cancer had heard of the healing service, and she came with her family. Father Bernie prayed over her. In November she went back to see her Catholic doctor. The bone cancer, a type that never goes into remission, was gone! All the cancer was gone!

That very month, the good doctor showed up at Father Bernie's healing service to see the man who could wipe out terminal cancer with one prayer to Jesus.

HEALING THE BLIND

It was 1983 on a cold Christmas night in a small ordinary town. Thirty people arrived at the evening mass at which Father Bernie was officiating. The day before, at Christmas Eve Mass, there had been a healing of a woman's eyesight. Father Bernie shared this good news with the congregation as he led the mass. All went normally during the service. He called out toward the end of the service for anyone interested in healing prayer.

One of the older parishioners came up and said, "I'll take some of that healing prayer. You know, I'm blind in my right eye. I can't see anything." Father Bernie laid hands on top of his head, prayed over him and blessed him. After about five minutes Father had him cover his left eye with his hand. Father Bernie held up two fingers.

"How many fingers are up?"

"Two."

"How many now?"

"Four."

"How many now."

"One."

"Wow."

A few days later, Father saw the man with glasses on. The man said to him, "Do you notice anything funny about these glasses, Father?" Father Bernie tried them on. The right lens was clear glass. He had 20-20 vision in an eye that had been totally blind.

Amazing Grace!

What an Awesome God he serves.

A WOMAN'S RETREAT

Father Bernie considered the healings in this story a level three miracle.

A woman's retreat with the theme of "The Holy Spirit" was being held at a large monastery style chapel. These women were not charismatic but knew Father Bernie was. The woman in charge asked him not to "freak them out."

He said, "Okay."

It was a huge chapel with a long, long aisle way. Father decided there would be one mass during the retreat on Saturday night. At that mass, there would be an anointing of the sick. Everyone would be eligible.

One woman there was using a walker with wheels. Another woman there was stooped over to a 90 degree angle. She had tiny short crutches. This woman's daughter and her best friend were there also.

Getting on into the evening, Father Bernie started performing the anointing of the sick. Both of the elderly women, the one with the walker and the one with the crutches came up to the altar. He prayed over each of them.

At communion time, Father noticed the woman with the walker had come up without her walker! When communion was over and before he closed mass, he went over to her and said, "I noticed you walked up without your walker. Would you mind stepping out into the aisle without your walker?"

She stepped out into the aisle.

Bernie told her, "I want you to walk all the way to the back of the church. "This was at least 120 feet or more. He went on to say, "I want you to walk all the way to the back of the church without hanging onto anything and no walker."

The women around him started to mumble, frown, and

talk in whispers. The lady agreed.

She started to walk without her walker. She had used it for years. Now, straight as an arrow she walked all by herself. Well, Father Bernie said the place hit the ceiling! Women were gasping, crying, even yelling! "Wheeww! Wheee!"

By the time she got to the back of the church, even she was crying. Father Bernie then said, "Now I want you to lift up your hands to God and give Him thanks and praise." Then he thought, "Oh, no, that's charismatic stuff."

But, she did it!

She raised her hands up, cried and thanked God. The other women whooped and hollered! Father Bernie went on saying, "Now, walk back." She walked all the way back by herself. He told her she did not need her walker anymore. He told the ladies he had also done this with people in wheelchairs. They too, had come right out of them. As far as he was concerned that night, he was done.

Then God spoke to Father Bernie, "DO YOU HAVE THE GUTS TO ASK THE STOOPED WOMAN TO DO THE SAME THING?" In other words, God wanted the elderly stooped woman to walk without her crutches or assistance too. He had a healing for her too, to be able to walk all the way to the front and all the way to the back, and back up to the front.

He thought, "Oh, brother. Well, I don't take credit for healing, and I don't take the blame if it doesn't work." So, he went and found her in her aisle. He said, "Now it's your turn."

"Aaaaahhhhh!!" Now all the women gasped with fear and expectation. They couldn't believe it! "You can't be serious!"

Fr. Bernie said to her, "Are you willing to come out and try walking all by yourself with no help all the way to the front, to the back, and up to the front?"

She said, "I'll try."

He took her by the hands and she came up out of her seat. She was still stooped over. Father Bernie then said to her, "You will never be able to walk stooped over because your center of gravity is off and you will fall. You have to stand up."

She tried a little.

"No, a little more."

She stood up a little more.

"No, a little more than that."

She stood up a little more than that.

Pretty soon she was standing straight up! The women around her were gasping and yelling. Her daughter couldn't believe it. Her mother had not stood up straight for years! And yet there she was, standing straight up in front of everybody!

Father Bernie continued, "Okay, now, you are going to let go of everything. I will walk with you. We are going to walk all the way to the back." She walked all on her own. She did not hang onto anything. She walked straight up.

Well, the place went up for grabs! Her daughter went completely berserk! Women were crying and screaming and yelling!

Father walked with her to the back. They turned around and walked all the way to the front. She did not hang onto anything. Then she went all the way to the back. Father told her, "You do not need your crutches anymore."

The whole time he was thinking, "I didn't think God would do it!" Remember, these women did not believe in the charismatic renewal.

The next day, the two women were not using their crutches or walker anymore. He met with them and used an open microphone to allow them to speak about their healings and express what they had gotten out of the retreat. Later a friend of hers said, "I've known Francis for 40 years, and I am an old woman. I have never seen anything like this in my life! And to the day I die, I am going to share with everyone what I witnessed here!"

Others around her knew this wasn't fakery. There were no dramatics. Father kept his calm and he let the women go berserk.

Father Bernie again stated at the end of the telling of this story, that this was still only a level 3 in the miraculous!

A PRIEST'S RETREAT

Father Bernie was asked to lead a priest's retreat. Unfortunately, it was a disappointment to him starting out. He was called to fill in at the last minute. The diocese was absolutely desperate to get someone. Their facilitator had cancelled at the last minute. Father told them, "You will have to take what you can get. I've never done a priest's retreat before."

"Okay."

They said that was fine, just come and help. Father Bernie thought doing a priest's retreat was serious business. It ended up looking more like "vacation time."

The man who called him, two days into the retreat came and told him, "Father, you are going too long and you are giving too much." Bernie thought to himself, "This is a bunch of crap." But he complied.

He shortened the length. He also cut some of the content. In short, Father Bernie was disgusted. He said in his heart, "This is the last time I will ever do a priest's retreat."

There were two priests there who were good friends, older men, who believed in Father Bernie's ministry. They came forward to talk with him. One said, "Father, we have a friend of ours, a lady who is going down hill fast. She has breast cancer. Would it be alright if she came here and you prayed over her?"

"Sure!"

On Wednesday she showed up. She was swollen and hurting. Her husband looked like death warmed over. Just as if he was going down the drain with her. As the wife went, he went. The husband admitted to Father Bernie that the night before was the worst night of her entire life. She went from being a very vibrant woman to being totally down. It was a pathetic situation.

Father Bernie led them into the chapel to pray. He knew there wouldn't be any priests in there to disturb them.

They sat down and got as comfortable as they could, and Father Bernie started praying. Her pain level started to go down. They prayed more.

"How are you feeling?"

"Better."

Father Bernie believed God was doing something, and He was going to do something more.

Now remember, he was still at the priest's retreat. They had started with 46 men and by Friday, they were down to 18.

On that Friday, the lady came back as well. Her energy had come back. Her swelling had gone way down. Her whole vibrancy had come back! She looked entirely different from Wednesday to Friday. Three days made a total difference.

She got up and witnessed before the priests that were there. Even the bishop heard of it and he believed it.

Fr. Bernie considered these to be level 3 healings.

MEDJUGORJE

Father Bernie stated he was in Medjugorje in 1987, a place he really didn't want to go to. This is his story of how God got him there.

In 1987, while at a local parish, Father Bernie was being "pestered" by a couple who had just come back from the Medjugorje shrine. They thought he should make a pilgrimage to Yugoslavia. It was not in his heart to go. But, after a time, he told them he would go back to the rectory and pray before a big creosote cross. (An 8 x 8 railroad tie size cross). He "put out a fleece". He said, "If I stand in front of the cross and the moon is on the other side of the cross, that's a sign from God and I'll go to Medjugorje."

Well, the moon was behind his back and he was facing the cross. He said to himself, "Good, I don't have to go to Medjugorje." As he was walking back to his rectory the Lord spoke to him. The Lord God said, "THAT'S NO SIGN. WRITE YOUR PROVINCIAL." This took him by surprise. But in obedience he wrote a letter that was not very encouraging. In fact, it was a pretty neutral letter. He expected to get a letter back saying something like, "It's not approved by the church, it's nonsense, etc." Father Bernie did not want to go to Yugoslavia. He reasoned, "The Blessed Mother is right here. Why should I have to go all the way over there?"

The provincial wrote back. He not only allowed Father Bernie to go but encouraged him to go! Father Bernie's reply was? "Aaaaahhhh!!" But what could he say? So he went.

While there, he met a couple who agreed with his ministry of healing. They started sending him people to be prayed over. *Everyone* they sent to him was healed!

Now the church had not yet given its official approval.

One of the laymen involved with Our Lady of Fatima was there. He was a Fatima Crusader, and they were adamantly opposed to Medjugorje because the pope had yet to consecrate it with the Bishops of Russia. And in their eyes, every disaster that was happening in the land was because this hadn't been consecrated yet.

This man and his wife came to see Father Bernie at 10:30 in the evening. They came to where Bernie was staying. He said to him, "Father Bernie, there is an Irish lady with bad knees. She has had to cancel all her visitations to the Marian shrine because she can't walk to them. Would you go over and please pray for her?"

"Alright."

Father Bernie went over to where she was staying. There was a courtyard there with a lot of people in it. It just so happened they met a Croatian man who lived in the United States. He spoke perfect English and perfect Croatian. The couple invited him to come along with them. Father Bernie prayed over the Irish lady. Her knees were healed in front of the Fatima Crusader and the Croatian man. Now, she could continue making her visitation to the Marian Center.

There was another man there, an Englishman. He also had bad knees. Father Bernie asked him if he needed prayer. The Englishman replied very stoically, "No, that's alright Father. You have more important things to do."

"Okay."

While Father was still making this pilgrimage, there was a set of grandparents living at the house where he was staying. They had a son who was married and had a little three year old girl. The grandmother asked through a translator, "Would you pray over my three year old granddaughter? She has never walked in her life." That was all they told him.

"Sure."

It was quite cool out and the little child had on several layers of clothing. The mother was holding her. They were all outside gathered around, the mother, father, the grandparents, Father Bernie, the interpreter and the little girl.

Father Bernie put his hand on the little girl's hair but she didn't like that. He then put his hand on her back. While they were praying he felt heat coming out of her back, through all the layers of clothing and into his hand! When they got through praying, through the translator, Father told the little girl's mother to squat down with her. He told the father to do the same. He was a little distance from his wife and daughter. Then, he told the father, to call his daughter.

The mother let go of the child and she waddled all on her own to the father. They all started crying. They all went into praising God. Everyone started shouting, "It's a miracle! It's a miracle!" Later on, the little girl was standing all by herself playing with the hair on her head. The grandmother started yelling in Croatian. The translator translated the grandmother's outburst. "Look! She could never do that before!" She had never even stood on her own.

Afterwards, Father Bernie found out the reason she had never walked before. At six months old, she had spinal meningitis. It eats away the myelin film around the spinal cord. All the electrical signals got shorted out going down the branch to the legs. The signals never got to the legs so she couldn't walk. She couldn't stand at all for three years before that day. Father Bernie continued his story, "When I felt heat go down her back that was God healing the myelin so fast that heat came out. And that's why she could walk now. Within five minutes, she was running

This was a level four miracle.

DELIVER US FROM EVIL

At Father Bernie's parish, there was a parishioner who once in a while got a sense that if Father Bernie would pray for a certain person, God would heal him. This man had a co-worker who was very seriously ill in the hospital when this sense came over him again. He asked Father Bernie to go pray over him. "Sure."

Father Bernie went with him to the hospital and they both prayed over the man. Sure enough, he got better after the prayer. This person came to Father Bernie again telling him that he met another person whose family member needed a healing. He was a deliverer of recapped tires.

Somebody he met on his route had a wife who had a spinal cord that kept producing fluid. The fluid built up and went into her brain. It put pressure on her brain causing her great pain and suffering. She couldn't even go out in the sun. Even though the doctors could do spinal taps, the body would not stop producing this fluid. There was nothing else they could do for her. Finally, her spinal cord could not be tapped anymore. She was going to die.

Her family brought her to Father Bernie late one evening. They were a half hour late, and Father was there waiting with another parishioner, Katie. When they finally arrived, the woman walked past Katie going into the church, and Katie felt something cold go past her. She said nothing to Father Bernie at the time.

They all went up into the sanctuary. This family was not Catholic. In fact, Father did not think these people were churchgoers. Of course, at the present moment, she could not have gone to church anywhere! She couldn't be out in the sunlight. They sat her down in a chair. Father Bernie started leading the prayers. Somewhere in the prayer, Father Bernie told satan to leave. Be gone. Both the male parishioner and

Katie felt something go through their body and out their feet. It was cold. This was some kind of a satanic influence.

At the beginning, she was hurting. When they were through praying over her, she didn't hurt anymore.

Father found out she had a doctor's appointment three days later on a Monday. She didn't show up. The nurse called her.

"Where were you?"

"I was out shopping."

"OUT SHOPPING? You can't be outside in the sunlight!!!"

She again said, "I went shopping."

That's it. She was healed!

Praise God!

LEVEL   FIVE

One night, Father Bernie and some others were praying in the sanctuary. It was a Sunday night prayer meeting, and they put on praise music for 45 minutes. Everyone was praising God, walking around and praying for one another. There were no official rules.

When it came time to pray over people, one of the parishioners had just had ear surgery. She sat down in front of Father Bernie. He asked her, "What do you want from the Lord?" She replied, "I'd like to be able to hear out of this ear. The doctor who did the surgery said I'll never hear out of this ear again." "Okay."

Father Bernie and several parishioners laid hands on this lady to pray. After they were through praying, it occurred to Father Bernie to test her for hearing. He told her to stick her finger in her right ear. Father started talking to her, and she said she could hear him.

Her doctor had said she would never hear again, and she said she could. Father settled on her word that she could. Father Bernie then told her to go back to her doctor, and tell him that she can now hear.

So, she did.

She went back to see him. She still had a large wad of cotton stuck in her ear. The doctor came in the room and he started to examine her, and she said to him,

"Doctor, I can hear out of my left ear."

He replied, "No, you can't."

She was insistent, "Doctor I can hear!"

Firmer he said, "NO, you can't."

"Doctor, I can hear!"

The doctor lost it saying, "No, you can't! I have removed your eardrum, and without your eardrum, you cannot possibly hear!"

"Well, I **can** hear!"

Exasperated, the surgeon took all the cotton and bandaging out of her ear. He took his otoscope and looked into the canal. Then, he set the instrument down and stopped. He went and got his partner and brought him into her room.

"Look at this. The eardrum is growing back."

Eardrums don't grow back, but hers did, and she most certainly could hear.

This is a level five miracle. There is no other way to explain this.

Regeneration is a level five.

A PERFECT JOB

This is a story that Father Bernie heard but was not there to verify. This is also a level five story.

There was an old nun making a retreat at Corpus Christi. She told Father she had a "hot line" with the Blessed Mother, and people knew about it. They would write to her to pray for this and that. She would then get on her "hot line" to the Blessed Mother and ask her to ask Jesus to heal those in need.

She was called to Medjugorje by the Blessed Mother herself. So she went.

The trail was very rough and this little old nun fell. Both bones in her lower leg broke and stuck out of the skin. Now she was in her 80's at the time.

Two men carried her in a "firemen's-carry" to get her off the mountain. They took her to her room and laid her down on the bed. Well, she got on her "hot line" to the Blessed Mother right away! She said to her, "You were the one who wanted me to come to Medjugorje! Whoa! Now I broke my leg! Tell Jesus he has to heal my leg!"

She was being very adamant about it. Of course, Father told her that once you are past 80, you can do that! After all, she was really hurting! She fell asleep praying.

When she woke up, she could walk. When she came back to the United States, her doctor x-rayed her leg. He then said to her, "Yes, it's obvious both bones were broken, but whoever set them did a **perfect job**!"

Isn't that something?
Isn't that our God?

A NORMAL HEART

Father Bernie has seen many miracles as a Chaplain at different hospitals over the years. This is a story of a fifth level miracle, before his ordination, that really touched my heart. And, I thought it would yours too.

Bernie was assigned to the surgical floor of the Cardiac Care Unit (CCU) at another hospital up north. As he went from room to room ministering to people, he came across a 50 year old male patient and his wife. He was quite ill, and in fact, he was dying at the time.

The wife took Brother Bernie aside and told him that her husband had just had eight heart attacks. He was hooked up to an IV unit with medication going into his vein that was literally keeping him alive moment by moment. She whispered that her husband would never make it home. But he did not know he was dying. Could Brother Bernie please pray for him? Of course, he said yes.

Later in the afternoon, Brother Bernie prayed for the man, while the wife left the room for a few minutes. Then, as the man spoke to Bernie, he told him that he did indeed know he was dying. He was just playing dumb so his wife wouldn't be upset. He then went on to say he was a Catholic and could Brother Bernie please pray for him.

And so he did.

In the middle of the night, the man's IV came out. The alarm went off!

Remember he could not go without this medicine in his veins even for a few minutes!

The nurse couldn't get the IV back in.

The doctor couldn't get the IV back in!

Chaos ensued!

But by that morning, all his readings were normal. They found nothing wrong with his heart. He went from dying to totally healed in less than six hours!

The hospital discharged him a few days later.

This was a level five miraculous intervention!

The hospital sent him home.

Praise God! Glory!

I'M FREE!

In the 1990's, Father Bernie was holding a Woman's Retreat on the west coast. There were about seventy women attending. As the retreat went on for several days, it got to be the day for the Sacrament of Reconciliation.

The last one to come in to the confessional was a woman in her mid-thirties. She did not like the way the retreat was going. She had a hardened heart. "Oh really?"

As they talked, he found out that she was a former Catholic and not been to confession in years. She was divorced and had been having a bad life, in general. After 45 minutes, she finished her confession, and it was time for Bernie to give the penance and absolution. He assigned her a penance asked her to say an act of contrition.

Then the Holy Spirit spoke to Father Bernie and said, **"Make an act of contrition up just for her. I'll give you the words!"**

And He did!

While Father Bernie was praying the act of contrition and she repeated it after him, her voice grew louder and louder. By the end she was yelling, "I'm free! I'm free!" Sobbing, she left the confessional. Then the Holy Spirit spoke again to Father Bernie. He said, **"Arguments and logic will not work. Only I can penetrate the heart!"**

Amen, and amen!

COME BACK!

A young girl in her early 20's brought a man with a severe speech defect to Father Bernie at one of his healing masses on a Sunday night.

Father Bernie was offering up prayer. This was for those who wanted to be prayed over and for anyone who wanted to join them in praying over people.

The people who wanted prayer came up and sat in wooden chairs. The ones praying for them would stand behind them, facing the crucifix.

The man came up for prayer. His speech defect so bad that you couldn't understand a word he said. Father started praying over him.

As Father Bernie was praying with his eyes closed he heard the Lord say, "TELL HIM TO SAY JESUS CHRIST I LOVE YOU." So Father told the man to look at the crucifix and say Jesus Christ I love you.

The man tried. "Gggrrrooollleeelllll."

"Say it again."

He tried again. "Jeeeesssuuuaiiillloooooouuuu."

"Say it again."

He tried even harder.

"Jeessuuussaiilllooovvveeuuu."

By that time you could tell it was English.

"Again."

Mustering up all his courage he said, "Jeessus, Iee llove you." And by the fifth time it came out! He cried with all his might, "Jesus I love you! Jesus I love you!"

It was plain as day. Perfect.

One woman at the service who had never witnessed a healing screamed out, "My God! He said Jesus Christ I love You!"

Father Bernie then told the man to "Lead us in the

Lord's Prayer."

And the man led everyone in the Lord's Prayer,   the "Our Father". His speech was totally restored! Not a dry eye was left in the house.

When the service was done, Father told the man to come back.

He would not.
His impediment came back.

SPIRIT OF EPILEPSY

This story is about a lady with a spastic colon who asked Father Bernie to pray over her for a healing. Even though he was not sure what that was, he thought it sounded pretty uncomfortable and that she needed prayer. So he did, and she was healed immediately.

When she came back the next day asking for prayer again, Father Bernie thought, "I don't pray over people twice for the same thing. It's like "double dipping." He will pray for someone three times at once but not three days in a row. The reason being is he has so many people waiting to be prayed for that he doesn't have the time. He said to her, "Weren't you here yesterday?" She replied, "Oh, yes. And I think I'm healed. No problems so far, but my husband has epilepsy, and his boss won't let him off work. Can I please sit in for him?"

Father Bernie said, "Sure! That's a different story!"

She got to sit in for her husband, Father Bernie prayed for his healing, and she went back home.

Five months later, he received a call from her. She said, "Father, I just wanted you to know my husband was healed of epilepsy. In a couple of days he will be at the lowest dose of Dilantin. I just wanted you to know he was healed."

These would be considered level three healings.

YES, JESUS LOVES ME!

Father Bernie had baked a cake for a raffle and a non-parishoner had been the winner. He called to notify her and in the background he heard a small child whimpering. Her little three year old was ill with a fever and was just lying around. She asked if he would mind praying for her? He was glad to do it. Could she put the little girl on the phone? She certainly could!

Father said, "Lisa, you aren't feeling well, are you?"

"Uh uh."

"Do you believe in Jesus?"

"Uh huh."

"Do you believe Jesus can make you feel better?"

"Uh huh."

"How 'bout I pray to Jesus right now and ask him to make you feel better?"

"Uh huh."

So he did. He said a little children's prayer. As he prayed he held his left hand out in front of himself and blessed the little girl over the phone. Then he told the child to give the phone back to her mother.

Within less than one minute he could hear her skipping and singing in the back ground! She was totally healed!

According to Father Bernie this was a level two healing.

SHORT STORIES

ONE

On one of Father Bernie's Mission Trips, there was a man who wanted to be a Eucharistic Minister. But, he had Parkinson's Disease so badly that he shook too hard to hold the host. Father Bernie prayed over him, and his shaking stopped immediately!

TWO

On another Mission Trip, a young lady with several children came up to him to be healed of dermatitis. She had to wear gloves when ever her hands were in hot water. The doctor's wanted her to have gloves on even when she was changing her baby. She was not about to do that! Father Bernie prayed a healing prayer over her.

The dermatitis went away, and she was healed.

THREE

A man was at a Charismatic get together and was healed of Tinnitus–a continual ringing in the ears, which he had had for many years. He had never talked about having it until he saw Father Bernie and was healed of it. Praise God!

SECTION TWO
LELAND AND ANNE SCHWARZ

"USED BY GOD UNAWARES"

Leland Schwarz
Retired Methodist Minister
Wife: Anne Schwarz, University chemistry professor
Born: April 6, 1937
Born in the Holy Spirit: 1978 under the Hunter's Group
His mission field: Since 1958 Suburban America
He walks in the Holy Spirit filled gifts of Miraculous Healing Spiritual Discernment and Words of Knowledge
He is an open vessel for the Lord.

Anne Schwarz
University chemistry professor
Husband: Leland Schwarz, retired Methodist Minister
Born: February 1, 1943
Born in the Holy Spirit: Five years old
Her mission field: Classroom/education
She walks in the Holy Spirit filled gifts of Words of Knowledge and Spiritual Discernment
She has no fear of death.
She is an open vessel for the Lord.

THE SINGAPORE INCIDENT
(Taken from Lee Schwarz's own writings)

In the spring of 1958, after a year studying at the University of the Philippines, I took a loop tour of South and Southeast Asia, including Hong Kong, Japan, Singapore, three places in India and Thailand. There was some touristy stuff to do, but I mostly visited people with whom our family had a connection. As a brash college kid, I invited myself to the home of F. Olin Stockwell, author of *With God in Red China,* a book which I had found powerfully compelling.

My visit was to be a single day, between the regular flight schedule from Singapore to Bombay. One of my college acquaintances was a Chinese fellow, Goh Kok Key, whose father was the Methodist Bishop of the Singapore Area. Stockwell and Bishop Goh had been estranged for years over policy differences at the seminary where Stockwell taught. My one day visit turned to two days because of mechanical problems with the airplane. This "coincidence" enabled Olin to invite the Bishop to dinner so he could meet and visit with me, the friend of his son. The real reason for the dinner, which I remember as the finest in all my travels about Asia, was to begin the healing of the relationship between these two formidable men, without either of them losing face.

God uses even the unwitting to accomplish His perfect will.

A LITTLE ONE

Almost 35 years ago, before Lee and Anne married, Lee was living in Logansport. He went on a drive with a young lady. During this time, she clearly got a headache. Lee noticed her facial expression and asked her if she had a headache. She replied, "Yes."

Without thinking, he reached over and put his hand to the back of her head and neck. She cried out, "Oh! What did you do?" He said back to her, "I massaged your neck a little." She replied, "My headache is almost gone!"

He broke the rule God gave to him about healing. She had not asked first. Lee said in response to this story, at the time, he was feeling his oats. And thankfully, God allowed it.

IN THE BEGINNING...LEE

Lee had always felt a close walk with the Lord. He came "under conviction" at a church summer camp during his senior year in high school. It was not an easy path to follow.

He felt since 1958 his ministry was for Suburban USA. The church hierarchy however was not in agreement with that. Lee was sent many a time to rural areas. For one reason or another, his seasons at these churches ended short. He was not more than four years at any location.

The battle between where God was sending him and where the official church sent him was finally too much for him to bear. His body and mind had a nervous breakdown. For 12 years, until 2002, he was in therapy. He learned of his own personality flaws and how to deal with them.

As he was healing on the inside with man's help, the Lord God Himself decided to get in on the act! During this time, Lee had a significant spiritual experience! This experience indicated to him, God's care can be trusted. Revelation and healing came forth at last! Alleluia!! When Lee preached, even if he had studied and made meticulous notes, there were times he was taken away by the Holy Spirit. When the Holy Spirit got involved, Lee would end up preaching on an entirely different subject than what he had prepared!

What is the reason for this? Someone in his congregation needed to hear the new words Lee was given to speak. He heard many times, "Thank you! I have been praying to hear just what you spoke on!" "That sermon was meant just for me!"

Lee is an open vessel for the Lord God. He is moveable and pliable to the Lord's commands.
Thank God!
Are you?

HOLY   SPIRIT,   COME!

In 1978, the year before Lee and Anne were married, Lee went to a series of meetings while at a church in Battleground, Indiana. It was led by the "Hunter's Group". They were charismatic teachers. The group consisted of a small support staff and a musical group. In these meetings, Lee was introduced to the active presence of the Holy Spirit. They met in an old Methodist church for several evenings.

On one particular night, every single person was slain in the spirit at the same time! There were over 300 people there. Not one of them was hurt while falling to the floor. Lee was watching row after row of people being laid down like wheat. When, all of a sudden he himself was looking at the underside of a chair! He had no memory of getting down onto the carpet!

Some of the people he went to the meeting with were life long smokers. During this meeting, they were cleansed body and soul. They never touched another cigarette for the rest of their lives. They were rescued.

Yes, rescued!

The last night of their meetings was when the fire fully fell. Everyone was all a chatter about all the healings they had seen over the last several days. They were now realizing any Christian can heal because it's not them, it's God. We are mere cooperative channels for the Spirit of God to move through.

At the end of the last meeting, Charles Hunter said to the group, "I want all pastors in the audience to line up in the front. Then all who have needs come up to a pastor and they are going to do what they have been taught. You are going to see and experience healings."

Well, Lee went up front shaking in his boots when the first person came up for prayer. He started praying and he saw something happen! People came up one by one. They told him what their problems were. Lee prayed for each one of them, believing he was being heard. As he was doing this, Lee could see what their problems were. He prayed about this with his hand on their forehead. (That was when Lee found out about "catchers", people who stand behind the person receiving prayer.) They were slain in the spirit, all but one man who was standing in for a person not at the meeting.

After all that occurred, God spoke to Lee's heart. God told him, "THIS IS THE WAY IT WILL ALWAYS BE. PEOPLE WILL HAVE TO COME TO YOU AND ASK YOU FOR HEALING." It then gives Lee permission to pray over them and get their healings.

This was the impartation Lee received.

Healing is by the hand of God for the glory of God! Lee is under the authority of God. He can only use his gift as directly permitted.

IN THE BEGINNING ANNE...

I have listened to Lee tell his wife's story over and over. Much of it will come out in her own book that she is currently writing. But, I do have permission to tell a small amount of her amazing life story.

Anne has great depths of spiritual insight. God has intervened for her life several times, and she has no fear of death. She has great perception and insight.

When Anne was five years old, her grandfather had been a "railroader" all his life. After retiring he lived with Anne and her family half the year and the other half he lived in Florida. By that time, he was very old and in poor health. Everyday for lunch Anne would climb up in Grandfather's bed to sit with him. They would have the most wonderful time visiting!

One day, she went up before lunch to sit with him. Grandfather said to the tot, "I want to tell you a story. One day Jesus will send a train for me. It will be full of angels. I am going to get on with the angels to go to Jesus. Now I don't want you to be sad. The adults will be sad, but I don't want you to be sad. Now go downstairs and tell your Mom and Grandma to come up and see me."

She hopped down from the bed, scrambled down the stairs and told her elders that Grandpa wanted to see them. So up the stairs and into his room the ladies went.

"Yes Poppa?"

"Poppa!"

As Anne promised her beloved Grandfather, she never grieved. She knew where he was. And because of this, she has no fear of death.*

* When Anne's Mother was 85 years old, she asked Anne about this story. She asked Anne if it was true. Anne replied, "Yes, Mom, every word of it."

LEFT: Deborah, Mark Anne and Lee in Bothel, WA having arrived safely after their seven day journey across America.

THE MEETING OF TWO HEARTS

In 1978, Anne came in to Lee's life at a CFO, "Camp-Farthest-Out", meeting. At the time Lee had been pursuing another lady. God told Anne to write a letter to Lee stating that he was to marry her. So she sent the letter to Lee and awaited his response. Lee took Anne's letter to the Lord. He asked Him what he should do.

The Lord God told him, "ANSWER QUICK, YES!"

Lee quickly got hold of Anne and said, "Yes, I am in agreement!" In one exchange of correspondence, they agreed to be married. That was in September of 1978.

Over the Thanksgiving holidays, Lee took Anne to meet his family. They took to Anne immediately and urged them to get married over the Christmas holidays. Oh, my! Anne was just finishing up teaching 200 students that quarter! Lee and Anne both had little time to plan the wedding and reception. But they agreed at the end of the year they would marry. Plus Anne made both her dress and her mother's. All done in one month's time! Whew!

Their planned New Year's Eve wedding ran smack into an ice-storm! A real "nor-easter"! By their happy day, there was one and a half inches of ice on the ground! Only one-third of the people could make it in. And they did have to change the date to January 1, 1979. Almost 33 years later, they still live in that moment. It taught them their first lesson, be flexible!

For reasons only known to God, the Schwarz's have never quite gotten money ahead. Whatever they had been able to save, something would always come along and take it. Something was always whittling away at their savings.*

The down payment for this new house they recently moved into, took the last of their nest egg. The way they saw things was that God had always taken care of them. They have always had "just enough." It seemed to be part of their walk of faith.

Let me remind them, and you dear readers, that the God we serve is the God of "more than enough!" We serve the same God that Jesus asked to feed the 5,000 men and had 12 baskets of food left over. More than enough!

*And may I again remind all of us of 2nd Kings 4: 1-7. This is where God took a family who feared the Lord, from poverty to wealth in 24 hours. They were given enough money to live on the rest of their lives. That is akin to one of us in our day as winning the lottery.***

God is definitely in the wealth/blessing/increase of his children, business. Alleluia!

** *Please note this author is not telling anyone to go out and buy a lottery ticket! If God wants to bless you monetarily, He will find a way to make sure you get the message and what to do with it.*

UNBINDING THE GOSPEL

Words of knowledge from Leland Schwarz

"Unbinding the gospel has to come from your heart and soul. This way you can learn how to talk to people about Jesus during ordinary circumstances. In this way people can be revitalized. This is real evangelism!"

"Be an apostle, an ambassador for Christ, an emissary. 2 Corinthians: 5 states "We are to live as disciples of Jesus". Use words as God directs you to. Trust God for the outcome and to fix problems."

"When we listen badly, God is still with us. He does not abandon us. The consequences may just be a little messier, that's all. There is **nothing** He can't fix!"

"There is a personal involvement in healing. People must be receptive. They must believe and trust. They must have no stoppers. The situation must be primed for the "Maximum Flow" of the Spirit of God to come through, and it will happen. ***Then, no force can stop it***. It may be only a momentary flow, but that is God wanting it at that moment!"

"You need to have people of faith together. The power of collective prayer, the unity of the mind, heart and spirit is remarkable. It opens a channel right to Heaven and you will feel the thrill of the Holy Spirit moving." *Lee knows with 100% assurance that God does what He says He will!*

When Lee is asked to pray over someone, he sees "God's gold" come down and enter the situation. Then everything changes. Even though he can perceive the movement of the Holy Spirit, often, he does not know the outcome. Lee does not feel the heat on himself.

He does this because God asked it of him. He says the same is for me. I do things because God asked. I am compliant. The outcome of each situation is as God intends. The results are left to God. We do what God asks, and then we move on.

"The theme of the Gospel of John is: the Kingdom of God is here in our midst and within each person who will receive it. Jesus is embodied directly into His people. We choose whether we accept and live in it or not. But if you accept it, then you are children of God, and the blessings that come with that birth right are a revelation unto itself! He is a Mighty God bringing mighty gifts!"

"In [the book of] Revelation, the battle continues. Yes, it is a continuous thing. We war against our own nature. As it was the same with Job, is still now with us. Remember, satan is still subject to God, and we are the children and heirs of God!"

Is there a battle brewing on earth? What is to come? This is beyond Lee's understanding. "Jesus said only the Father knows the time. But the key is faithfulness. Not in the future, not in a rapture, but now, for the here and now."

"When we are in a state of oneness with the heart of God, the mind of God, the will of God, then we will love like God. We are called to be the love of God to this world."

"We are to tend faithfully and steadily learn. Our faith is to be childlike with mature decisions. We are to walk by faith even if in the middle of a situation we have confusion on which way to go. When you come to the end, you will say yes."

When Lee gets knowledge, it bubbles up inside him. He receives moments of clarity. *[Me too.]*

"Healings are to demonstrate the glory of God and to demonstrate the presence of His Kingdom in the here and now. How do regular Christians get to this? ***Go do what your religion prescribes.*** Catholics, Baptists, Methodists, Evangelicals, Pentecostals, etc., we all have different ways of access to God."

MY INTRODUCTION TO THE SCHWARZ'S "SAINT ANNE"

About fifteen years ago around 1996 when I was still in nursing school, one of the classes I had to take was chemistry. "CHEMISTRY! I hate chemistry! I suck at it!" I cried. Now in my defense, I was good at biology. I could do it all day long. But when it came to chemistry and lab work, my brain went to mustard.

The semester began with my new teacher introducing herself and her husband, who was her assistant. She wrote her name on the chalk board.

"Anne Schwarz."

Before I could think my hand went in the air, waving back and forth. I was thinking in my head, "Important knowledge, important knowledge!" What I said out loud was, "Oh, oh, oh!!"

"Yes, you have a question about my name?!"

I offered, "Do you know who Anne with an "E" is? Do you know who you are named after?"

Husband and wife eyed each other. Anne replied, "No, who?" Jubilantly I said, "That is St. Anne, Mary's Momma and Jesus' Grandma, Patron Saint of Grandmother's."

Now Anne was smiling. She said with genuine warmth, "Thank you! I never knew that!"

"You're welcome!"

It was a small beginning to a beautiful relationship.

And my, oh my, what was to come!

SECOND DAY OF CLASS

I went to medical assistant and nursing school on government assistance. I was a newly divorced woman with three little boys to take care of. The point here was all my education, books and supplies were paid for by Pell Grants and Vocational Rehabilitation.

When I went to my second day of chemistry class and Anne said we would not be using the standard book but one she had written, and it would be $20.00, my heart sank. She went down each row, gathering necessary funds to put in the book order.

Then she got to me.

I started, "Uh, I would like to borrow someone else's book if you don't mind." I had no money at all and really didn't care to share that information with the whole class.

Anne replied, "We really think you are going to need a book. Sharing would not be advisable."

Now I had to tell. Rats. In front of everyone, my self-esteem wilted as I confessed, "Well, see, I am here on grants and they won't pay for any more books this semester. I already sold my home to go to school. I don't have anything left to give you."

"You sold your home?"

"Yes, ma'am, I sold my and my children's home."

"Oh."

The next week when the new books came in we were to start learning in earnest. All the books were given out, names were assigned to them and class was ready to start.

Anne started the class with this statement, "We will take a short recess before we get started. Be back in ten minutes. "Miss Aubrey, may we see you outside?"

I was thinking, "Oh, boy. This is it. They are going to tell me I can't take the class without her book. And without this class, I can't graduate and get a job and support my children. Twenty dollars is standing between me and a life for my children! Help me Lord!"

Heart pounding, I stepped outside and waited to hear what my teachers had to say. We walked outside, and I turned to face them and waited. Lee took from behind his back a book and handed it to Anne who handed it to me.

Stunned, I said, "I still don't have any money to give you."

"We know."

"Why are you doing this?"

"We are doing it because you sold your children's home to go to school."

FYI: I tried as hard as I could in that class to thank them for their generosity. Lee was my tutor, who helped me in my struggle to succeed. And in the end, when I received my report card, I got a "B."

I called Anne at home right away. "Where's my "C" that I actually earned," I asked. Anne replied matter of fact, "In all my years of teaching, I have never seen someone try as hard as you. Effort counts too."

She's right, you know, and your effort counts too. Don't give up. Whatever battle you're in, don't give up.

A CLOSELY GUARDED SECRET

During all the time I knew Lee and Anne as teachers and educators, I did not know of Lee's special gift of healing or of Anne's insightful nature. It wasn't until several years later, as we became close friends that I was allowed to find these things out, much like you would when you peel an onion back one layer at a time.

After class was over, the next fall semester I fell down the steps of my two story townhouse and fractured C-6, C-7 cervical vertebrae, thus ending my nursing studies. The school wanted me to get on a waiting list of two years to get back in. Anne was furious!

Mark and I made the decision then that we could wait no longer to get married. As soon as my annulment was decreed, we sent out announcements. To our delight, Lee and Anne came to our wedding. This time, it was dear Anne who had her arm in a sling from an accident. She was healing nicely, though.

We saw them many times over the next several years as we drove back and forth to each other's homes. Mark even took on being their private landscaper. For two years running the Schwarz's lawn care was our pet project. What fun adventures we all had together!

The fall of 2004 brought a disaster into my life with a fracture of LL5-S-l, lower back. It was during this time, the "onion layers" started peeling back and I got to see the real Leland and Anne Schwarz in action.

This is our story together.

A CHRISTMAS MIRACLE

[This excerpt is from the book titled "Walking in the Supernatural", published 2011 by Home Crafted Artistry and Printing. Re-issued under the new title "Miraculous Interventions" published 2012 again by Home Crafted Artistry and Printing.]

In the beginning of our third year of marriage, Mark and I had several people who were not acquainted with each other, come forward to tell us that we were to go look for land, build a home and even who our builder would be. Since we do not believe in coincidence, we started early in the new year of 2002 looking for land. I wrote on a piece of paper "$18,000.00" and "for sale by owner." That is how we would know the land when we saw it. Mark even got the feeling of where we should drive. When we stepped onto the land, the Holy Spirit fell on me from my feet up. That's it. We were home.

By the fourth year of our marriage, and two years into our new home, my back was damaged, it fractured at LL-5, S-1.

We had no health insurance. The muscles along the left sciatic nerve from the gluteus medias to the Achilles tendon froze. It felt like a charley horse 24 hours/seven days a week. All the doctor could do was put me down with medication. From the pain, my temperature would go up to 100 degrees, and my hair fell out in clumps. My blood pressure rose week after week.

During Thanksgiving week, after seven weeks of incredible pain, I laid on the floor at 3am and cried out to the Lord, "I know you are God. You can do anything! Take me up! Get me out of here! Take me home! I don't want to be here anymore! You can do it! I don't want to be a wife or mother anymore!" My husband was on the floor next to me rebuking every word out of my mouth. Our youngest son, Andy, was hollering in the hallway, "Momma, stop it! You are scaring me!"

It was then I heard a voice as if someone was standing next to me. I believe an angel said, *"Hang on! Your Christmas Miracle is coming! Your Christmas Miracle is Coming!"* Being in the frame of mind I was in, I cried out again, "Christmas! It's not even Thanksgiving!" With my next breath I said, "But not my will but thine be done." My husband rubbed anointed oil on my back and leg and prayed over me for two hours. I was finally able to get back into bed and sleep a little while until my next round of medicine was due.

While this was going on, I played praise music over and over again until I wore out the CD.

My doctor scheduled me for an epidural block. It was Christmas time, and my husband Mark was a bench jeweler. He was pressed for time and had no time to stay and help me afterwards. He took me over to the hospital that morning and the nurses prepared me for the procedure. The head nurse in charge of me blew the right vein three times trying to put in an IV for medication distribution.

When they finally got me ready and wheeled me back to the operating room, the anesthesiologist ran the medication down the wrong leg two times! By this time, I had bilateral inflammation and pain on both sides!

Mark brought me home, and my good friend Margaret stayed with me and cooked us a lovely beef stew as she waited for the next round of people who came to help. My cousins came and brought us dinner. By that time I was in terrible pain. I was breaking out in a cold sweat, and started to moan and yell. Gail told me as she was leaving our home, "Deb, you aren't praying hard enough! I'll be praying for you."

The next day my dear friend Mary came and stayed the whole weekend with us. She cooked meals and did dishes, made cookies, and brought me some wholesome treats. Anything that might cheer me up, she did. We prayed together and cried together. She took wonderful care of me. Mark owes a debt here he can't repay. It took all the stress off of him. The day Mary had to go back home, our friends Lee and Anne called. They wanted to come and see us the next evening. It was soon to be their 25th wedding anniversary, and they wanted Mark to make Anne an opal ring for her present. It would be very nice to see them.

The next morning while praise music was playing, I was laying on the floor trying to wrap a few Christmas presents for our children. All of a sudden I heard beside me, "Be very sorry for everything you have ever done."

I took off my glasses, put my head on the floor and cried for half an hour before the Lord. I had a repentant heart. I did not understand that I was being prepared for what was to come.

When they arrived that evening I was laying back in a recliner. I was sweating with pain. Anne conducted her business with Mark quickly then she came over and sat on the couch by her husband and took a good look at me. She said, "Debbie, you look terrible."

I replied, "I know Anne, but I keep hearing somebody next to me saying over and over that my Christmas miracle is coming. I believe I am going to have a miracle sometime this season!"

Anne got really excited and grabbed Lee by his arm. She said to him, "Lee, did you hear that? Debbie is going to get a Christmas miracle! We believe in that too!" Then she looked at me and said, "Lee's hands are anointed like the apostles." I knew right then and there my time for full healing had come. Lee and Anne looked at each other. She said, "You have to ask him in faith."

I asked Lee, "Would you please allow the Holy Spirit to enter you and heal me?" He said, "Why sure!" as if I had asked him to go get me a glass of milk.

Mark and Lee gently laid me on the floor. All I could see were knees. Mark was on his knees at my feet. Anne was sitting on the couch beside us, and Lee on his knees at the middle of my back. He said to me, "Debbie, say a prayer in your head. I will know when to start."

In my head I said, "Lord, I come before you humbly. Please find nothing in me that would cause you to turn away." He put one hand on my head and the other hand started down my back without touching me. He was inches above me. Immediately I felt heat. It felt hotter and hotter, until he got to the place that was damaged. I was yelling, "Hot! Hot!" Anne was giggling on the couch. She knew what was coming!

Then the damaged disc area began to tingle, to incite as if it were waking up from a sleep. The nerves were firing up! The left lateral muscle LL-5/ S-1 moved back in place. I *felt* the disc heal, wiggle and move back into place. Lastly, the right lateral muscle moved into place as well. At that point, Lee put his hand on my back and it felt like a "surgeon closing from surgery." All the pain ended. It was gone. Lee sat back. In an instant I jumped up all by myself! I could've flown! I yelled, "Yyyyiiiippppiiieeee!!" Then I started to cry.

We all started to cry. Mark cried out, "Praise the Lord!"

It was an instantaneous miracle! I looked up at Lee and asked, "How can this be?"

All of a sudden it felt like 2,000 years ago as he replied, "Woman, your faith has saved you."

I asked him again, "What did it feel like when the Holy Spirit entered you and healed me?"

He said he felt tremendous joy. He told me that I had no stoppers and that my faith was complete.

Now, I could stand and sit again. We laughed and cried. Like Peter's mother-in-law after she was healed by Jesus, I got up and served people drinks and snacks. It was the least I could do. The fracture was healed and I knew my sins were forgiven. What a glorious day!

I couldn't speak a whole sentence for three days. I was overwhelmed. My muscles were tired due to the stress of what they had been through, and I did physical therapy in my home with a book we found on line as my guide. The next day I could dress myself and drive once again. I could walk by myself.

Three weeks after my healing, I was lying on the family room floor doing my daily physical therapy, and I was cold. There was a draft coming in from the patio deck doors. From my side view, I saw a man in white pick up my blanket off the couch, bring it over and lay it on top of me.

I said, "Thank you." No one replied because no one was there. I went down the hall. Andy was in his room doing homework, and Mark was in our bedroom working on book work.

I tell you, it was an angel sent to comfort me after all I had been through. God, being no respecter of persons, if He will do this for me, what will He do for you? Evidently, all we have to do is ask, and be ready to receive.

THE ROAD TO SEATTLE
or
THE SEARCH FOR GOD'S SENSE of HUMOR!

When I first met Lee and Anne, they were living in Corydon, Indiana and I was living just outside of Jeffersonville, Indiana. Within the first two years we flipped communities! They moved to Jeffersonville, and I moved to Corydon with my new husband, Mark and our three sons.

Many a time we spent at each other's homes listening to or telling stories of God's marvelous love and perfect timing. We saw illnesses erased and broken bones immediately mended, and that was just on me!

Mark and I were their private gardeners. We also spent several Epiphany Christmas holidays together. (This is when the wise men came to the Holy Family and presented gifts to the baby Jesus). We together, were our own little unique family.

That is until Anne's soybean allergy got the best of her, and they decided to move out of the region. In fact, they needed to move from Jeffersonville, Indiana all the way across three time zones! Anne had been offered a position at a university in Seattle, Washington. This posed a problem. How were they going to get their son, all their stuff, and all their vehicles 2,500 miles?

Now, in my defense, it was Christmastime, and I was feeling particularly magnanimous, and helpful, and, well. . . I got carried away in the moment! Before my husband could stop me, Anne and I were jumping up and down squealing, "Oh! Won't it be fun? We'll call it Wagon's West! It will be an adventure! Why, Mark can just take off all his vacation time to do this!"

"WHAT?"

I heard my husband from across the room. His jaw

dropped. "Oh, honey. Anne says we can go with them to Seattle and help them move! Won't it be a fun adventure?" I smiled ever so sweetly.

The poor man gulped. He was in a tight spot. Everyone was looking at him and smiling in agreement with me. They were ready for his nod of approval. Finally, it came. Later, I had to promise him on my most solemn vow to never volunteer him for something without asking him first again! (We'll talk later about how many times I have broken that most solemn vow).

A few days later our good friends from across the pond, in England, Dave and Dianna Getting, called to wish us a Happy New Year. It was then that I got to share my new exciting news with them!

Well, not to be out done, Dianna turned to her husband and said, "I want to go on Wagon's West too!" Wonderful! It was settled! We could use a couple more drivers on the road.

Over the winter months, we went to the Schwarz's from time to time to help them sort and pack. Some boxes came to our home, some went to the Salvation Army, some went for a yard sale, some went to their church in Jeffersonville, and the rest got packed into two 25 foot long moving vans! Brother!

Winter soon melted into spring, which sprang into summer. July, our appointed time for saddling up, was fast approaching. Andy, our youngest son, was to spend two weeks with his best friend Tyler and his mom, Karen. Our other two boys already lived independently, but they agreed to watch over our home place until we got back.

The day finally came to leave, and Mark and I arrived at their house early that morning. We were to meet our friends from England up in Minnesota the next day. The two moving vans had already come and gone from the Schwarz's. All we had to do was get their 20 year old motor home, van and their son's car from one end of the country to the other. Saddles up! We hit the road from Jeffersonville and high tailed it north. From Minnesota, we would pick up our friends and head west.

Unfortunately, it did not turn out the romantic trip I thought it would be.

After several years of crying, praying and releasing emotions, I could finally see the humor in many of the situations we encountered.

What situations were those?
Why these of course.

I realize this is a book about miracles. I ask my Readers, at this time during this series of stories, please sit back and have a good time. The term "miracle" is used very loosely on the way to Seattle.
Thanks,
Author.

We had been promised for our help, the cost to us would be minimal. It ended up being all our savings. But, what were several thousands of dollars between family and friends? That was what I got for thinking in my head, "free two week vacation!"

Oh, and then there was the resort Mark, Dave, Dianna and I were to stay in for two nights. Let's see, how did that story go?

I remember now . . .

RESORT

We were into the end of our second day on the road trip when there was trouble with the 20 year old motor home that Lee was driving. We ended up being hours late picking up our friends David and Dianna, who sat waiting at a small airport with nothing to do but wait on us. Hopefully, I thought, this would not be the start of things to come.

Finally by 1 am, we arrived at our first real destination, the resort and campground. Lee, Anne and their son stayed with friends in the area, an elderly couple, while the four of us, Mark, Dave, Dianna and I followed the gentleman to his favorite resort. We parked next to each other, and he walked us to our room. We opened the door on the hot early July morning to stale air in a room with no air conditioning. There was one king size bed for our friends, the Gethings, and where were we to sleep? We went up the ladder (not stairs, l-a-d-d-e-r) to a four inch deep piece of foam bed. There was no air, no pillow, no bed, no nothing.

I turned to the elderly gentleman to say "No way," but he was already gone! Seeing that I was less than thrilled with the accommodations promised, he got out while the getting was good! We were trapped like mice at 1:30 in the morning!

We all made the best of it through the night. Well, everyone but me. Up and down the l-a-d-d-e-r I fussed going to use the small bathroomette. By 6:30 that morning I could take it no longer. The lodge where the big breakfast was being prepared had people moving around in it. There was my chance! I ran up to the door and knocked politely.

The ladies inside smiled politely back and said, "We don't open for another half hour!" I would have none of that. As hard as I dared I knocked on the glass, BAM! BAM! BAM! I was a force to be reckoned with!

"Open the bleeping door!"

Those sweet, plump, elderly women ran quickly to unlock the door. I'm sure they reasoned it must have been an emergency! Before they could get any words out, I ordered in my outside voice, "**Phone book! NOW!!**"

It was produced thin-air immediate.

Off I ran to the van we were driving, phone book and cellular phone in hand. All I wanted was the name of a hotel that I recognized to call. Alleluia! There was one in the area. I called and cried to the first human I got on the phone. I told him the whole story from my view point. The hours on the road, the break down, then, no air, no stairs, no bed, etc... "Help us please!" Help us he did!

"We're just a few miles away from you. Take down directions, and I will have two rooms prepared for you. I will only charge you for one night, and I will make sure there is a hot breakfast waiting for you when you arrive!"

"Thank you, dear sweet wonderful man!" A cry in the wilderness answered.

I ran to our room, threw open the door at 7 am and cried out, "**Get up**! Pack your bags! I got us a room at a great hotel with wonderful accommodations! He's only charging us for one night, and a hot free breakfast is waiting for us! Our rooms are being prepared right now! Move!"

Ten minutes later we were on the road.

After we all had our bellies full and slept another five hours on real mattresses, we called our friends to let them know of our change in hotels. Nothing further was said. And the two days we spent sight seeing were actually quite enjoyable.

But folks, we were not in Washington State yet.

During this seven day trip to the coast, we got to see *beautiful*, majestic sites all over the American North West. The song is rightly called "America, the Beautiful." It simply is. Canyons, mountains, rivers, fields of corn and soybeans feeding the world, it all took my breath away! National Monuments, Native American monuments, the Columbia River Gorge, and Wall, South Dakota, - now there's a story to tell! . . . and a picture is worth a thousand words . . .

AMERICA THE BEAUTIFUL!

BOOTS IN THE WALL

Wall, is a historic old west town. Its claim to fame is that it is still standing. There is a huge old fashioned mall of stores there. It was a real treat just to walk through and look around. They'll feed ya' ice-creams as big as your head! Truth!

When we first drove into town, I suggested since it was the Fourth of July, that we should go ahead and get a room somewhere before stopping and eating dinner. The Schwarz's assured me we would be able to get a room later that evening. So, off we went after a cook out dinner to the local old west mall. And we all had a great time!

I bought Mark a pair of real cowboy boots and a Stetson hat. My goodness, he was handsome in his attire! Dave and Dianna shopped for items to share with their family back home in England.   At the end of the evening, we all got ice-creams and started the search for a couple of rooms.

After an hour of calling around, we found one room. It was a 1950's motel. It had one double bed, just enough for Dave and Dianna and one twin bed, just enough room for Mark and myself to squeeze in. Lee, Anne and their son slept in the motor home.   The room had a little kitchenette with a table and four chairs, as well as a bathroom and the one bedroom. As we all started to nod off, that was when the giggling started.

First it was Dianna, and then it was me. Between giggles, Dianna said, "Those cowboy boots better stay in that box! No hanky panky!"

I laughed until my side hurt! How could she have seen inside my head? As close quarters as we were, the rooms had air conditioning, and we all had beds.

ABOVE: Mark and his famous "Wall" boots!

RIGHT: The little bungalow where we stayed one night.

COLUMBIA RIVER GORGE

To our good fortune, we never ran into bad weather all across the U.S., unless you consider the 80 mph winds whipping across the Columbia River that stopped us for the night.

We stopped on the ridge overlooking the Columbia River Gorge. Being late at night, we could not see the river below, but we sure could hear the rushing water beneath us. The winds traveling through the area were strong enough to knock a tractor trailer over the side of the bridge! No one was crossing that baby that night!

I tried to walk from the van to the little local gas station where we had stopped. The winds were so strong they took my breath away. I ran for the building to meet my friends inside. When I got inside, my friends had just made a reservation for the only room left in town, again. It was one large room with three double beds, a bathroom, and a small kitchen. It was over the laundry mat. Any port in a storm will do. At least we all had beds. Lee and Anne's son was again assigned to the motor home.

We drove our vehicles the two blocks to the side of the building. We got out whatever was necessary for the night. We walked up the stairs and into a spacious living and bedroom area. Other than a bit stuffy, it was okay. The guys opened a few windows for a time to cool things off, and the women of our group arranged a quick service meal. In other words, we all emptied our food stashes and spread it out on the table to share! It was one of the most fun times we had had so far during our trip. A sleep over! We had a sleep over!

As the night was coming to a close, we each one got ready for bed in the bathroom. Then we all told stories one after another until we fell asleep.

That was when the trouble started.

Lee fell asleep first, and then he started snoring. Anne belted Lee on his side and quipped, "Lee, your snoring is keeping us awake!"

We burst into giggles. Then it happened again and again. Laughter ensued. Then Annie fell asleep. In perfect unison, the two of them raised the blankets with their noise.

At first, it was funny, but when it kept the rest of us awake, we got seriously grumpy. Even the usual chipper Dianna let loose some good old fashioned American slang, of which I will not repeat here.

By four in the morning with cotton stuffed in our ears, Mark and I marched out to the van and slept in the front seats, and we slept there until dawn's early light. David came out shortly after that to let us know the "snoring fest" had come to an end shortly after we left for the van. They didn't have the heart to come and tell us.

"Thanks for that information. I think we will jump off the bridge now."

"Sorry, old pals," he quipped, "you are not getting out of this adventure that easy."

It was one more day's journey until we arrived at our final destination.

Washington State, here we come!

Mt Ranier rising up in front of us like a sleeping giant!

AT LAST!

All the sites and sounds of the areas we passed through were spectacular. But the best site of all was the long awaited Bothel, Washington. Lee and Anne would finally get to step inside their new home, and we would be in a hotel for more than one or two days for rest and recovery. We got our friends settled into their new residence. That evening, the Schwarz's thanked the four of us by taking us out to dinner at a very nice restaurant. They had a piece of chocolate cake that was seven layers high! Everything was forgiven! Bad times on the road were long forgotten.

We left our friends to do their unpacking, and the four of us went back to our hotel and rested for a couple of days until we figured out what to do next. We had all planned to rent a car and travel back through the south west states that we had not seen yet. Then, two things happened to change our minds.

First, we called everywhere to rent a vehicle, and no one wanted to rent to us going all the way across the country! It was going to be more expensive to drive than to stay in Seattle, sightsee and fly home.

The other thing was that I started my cycle one week early that very afternoon. I went straight to bed with cramps and tears. There was no way they could've got me in a car for seven days. Not in that condition! Our last week there, Mark, David and Dianna spent their time sight seeing and I spent it curled up with a heating pad and Advil. What's that saying, "All good deeds never go unpunished?"

The flight home was an eleven hour trip. Eight hours of it was in the air. Our plane ran into turbulence crossing over the mountains. The pilot came over the speaker and was very professional about it. "Please fasten your seat belts. We are experiencing turbulence. We are going over the mountains."

However, I cried out, "Jesus, Jesus, Jesus!"

Every time we hit an air pocket, I yelped. The dear Christian people behind me gently sang Christian bravery songs to shore me up. I thanked them for their generous spiritual support.

By the time we landed in the Louisville airport after 11:00 pm, I was physically and emotionally worn out! Weak kneed, I got off the plane, and Mark had to carry all of the luggage. He still beat me to the car of our friends who came to pick us up. I have not flown since.

What was the miracle in this long story I've told? No one threw me out of the van. No one threw me off a bridge. No one threw me out of the plane!

And all my friends forgave me, for my whiney, fretful, ungrateful, and unsportsmanlike conduct. Why, I even forgave myself. Hey, little miracles count too!

WAGONS WEST HO!!
SADDLE UP!

*PREVIOUS L: Mark & Dave Chamberlain, SD. R:
Mitchell Corn Palace, Mitchell SD – All of it is made
of corn!
BELOW Top L: Native American Monument
Top R: Badlands, SD.
Center: Mt Rushmore, SD
Bottom R: Trading Post in Wall, SD
Bottom L: God's Majesty!*

Vantage, Washington State, near the Columbia River Gorge (early morning)

LEFT: We called this a view of the "American West Pyramids"

BELOW: Natural Scenes out West

TOP: Two pictures at a local university in Washington state.

Left: David and Dianna in Seattle WA.

BELOW: Landscaping Lee and Anne's new home.

*Dessert at last!
Seven layers,
too!!*

*MontanaBig
Sky country.*

*`You can see
a hundred
miles!*

96

THE HAND OF GOD

This story is taken straight from the e-mail Lee sent me while we were corresponding about this book. As I wrote his stories about miracles, a series of them unfolded right before our very eyes. This all took place over the span of ten days. Sometimes in life, events happen as if all intertwined by a beautiful golden thread. As if the hand of God was and is still moving across the waters. Lee wrote:

We have more stories about God's Intervention than you know about. And they happened in the last week. As you know, Anne was scheduled for surgery July 12th to replace her terrible right knee. The surgery coordinator from the hospital called last week and said, "And you will be one of the very first patients in the new hospital wing." Tilt. Did she mean as in new carpets and new everything? A sniff test was in order. So, last Friday we went to the hospital for a sniff test. Sure enough, it was $500M, 12 floors of new carpet and plastic. It wasn't too bad as we walked into the wing. It was not too bad on the 10th (orthopedic) floor with all the empty rooms. Then, down the hall to the other end where there were a couple of rooms with a couple of beds in them, WHAM! Like a heart attack it hit Anne: her lungs were on fire, the chest pain was intense, her lungs were shutting down. The ER was not an option since it was in the same building.

Anne escaped the building, got to the car and took an Advair puff. She quickly returned to normal. We placed an emergency call to her pulmonologist who saw her on Monday.

Anne's doctor listened to her lungs. She said, "Surgery is off. There is no way we can keep you alive for the three days. You'll need to be in the hospital, and there is no place else you can get on the schedule this summer and be back in the classroom by September. By the way, where do you live?" Anne told her. The doctor replied, "Living there, you are constantly at a subclinical level of poisoning. That is why you react to everything else much too strongly. You have to move."

Move instead of surgery.

Ri-i-ight.

Well, at God's insistence we had agreed to rent a house a month ago and put our home on the internet. Within 24 hours we had a call on the home, but the rental deal fell through. So, we took our home off the internet. Last Sunday, the same woman who had called about the place a month ago, called asking if it was still for sale. Conditionally, yes. We visited awhile over the phone and she told me her family had recently put her father in a nursing home and had to sell his house.

"Oh? Where?"

"Snohomish." (Our target city)

We asked for the address and what the home was like. So, it went like this.

Friday: Emergency
Sunday: House talk.
Monday: Told we must move.
Tuesday: Looked at the house.
Wednesday: Met with the realtor at the house.
Thursday: Accepted our offer at 20% below the asking price.
Friday: Loan application finished.
Saturday: Met with the inspector.

While I was at the bank needing to know how to make out the earnest money check, the realtor called me. While I was talking with the realtor who needed to know the time frame for the inspection, the inspector called me with the answers to the realtor's questions!

Now, we still need to sell this place, but after all the above, do we trust God for the outcome? You bet! A couple of months ago, as we were all in a dither about moving or not moving and the surgery, I was in prayer about it all. God said to me then, "I HAVE THE ANSWER. I *AM* THE ANSWER."

Ya think?
Blessings,

Lee

ANOTHER LITTLE ONE

Thirty-five years after the little incident with the lady with the headache*, I came under attack while talking to Lee coast to coast. I was still taking notes for his portion of this book.

The first thing readers need to know is that I am not prone to headaches. It had to be a big flu or sinus infection to get me, and you can name those times in the last five years on one hand. I'm covered by the blood of Jesus, you know.

As Lee and I were talking, a headache came over me fast from the top of my head down through my neck! I felt a temperature coming on as well! "What's this?" I queried in my own head. I told Lee what was happening as I put a thermometer in my mouth. Lee went quiet to ask God Himself what was up.

Two minutes into this time frame, **fire** hit the left side of my brain. It went left to right. I took off my glasses. My temperature had gone down to 97.7 degrees. I got better minute by minute until fully healed within a few minutes.

I told Lee what happened to me and asked him what he saw. What he saw in his head was a **red, angry, painful, pathologic owie!** He saw my pain and told it to leave.

Then he saw *Blue, soothing, healing, peaceful.* The attack and the attacker had left immediately. That's just like Jesus, our example. Glory!

* See story "A Little One" on page 61.

THE THRILL OF HIS PRESENCE!

On several occasions Lee has felt the movement of the Holy Spirit. He feels the thrill of the Holy Spirit's presence and activity. This has always been confirmed by his wife, Anne. He usually asked Anne if she sensed something, and it is always the affirmative.

During the few weeks of these phone interviews with Lee, he was praying for a woman in the park. She and her husband were a spiritual couple that Lee had met, and she was going blind. Lee laid hands on her eyes, and he felt the moving of the Spirit of God. The lady told him her sight was immediately better! And another person who was there said his sight was better too!

Lee prays for people in the spirit, in church, daily life, anywhere really. Sometimes he goes to his prayer language. He does this when he is moved to do it or is asked to do it.

How grateful I am that God blessed my life with these two amazing people.

READ THE BOOK!

Have you ever wondered how others see you? Or have you ever wanted to see yourself the way others see you? If so, write a book about your life, and hopefully you will see God's impact on the situations you've experienced. The people who really love and understand you will line right up with you and be proud of your accomplishments, just the way Lee and Anne did for me. Lee's words to me and Anne's vision of what they saw when they read "Miraculous Interventions," left me speechless.

He said, "Deb, it was neat! It was like reading a "Life's Little Instructions" book. It shows clearly how you and Mark have walked with God over the years. It was neat how it all happened, the big and the small."

They loved the stories about how we met people along our path, inspiring them and helping them along their way. They also loved how I have the ability to touch people in a deeper way than other people would. I am in touch with the Holy Spirit of the living God, so I can touch their spirit as well. I have been blessed to see good, valuable and godly in each person. Again, he told me, I have no stoppers in my faith walk.

Wow! Thanks.

This came from a man and a woman who walk deep in the presence and spirit of God Himself, and they don't know how to be any other way.

A WEEK OF DREAMS FOR LEE

In one of our last phone conferences for this book, Lee asked me for my interpretation over several dreams he had recently had.

I replied, "Shoot partner."

Lee started, "It was the first week in August. I had three days of dreams. They were really vivid. See what they tell you. In the first dream I was in the field of business. I was getting ready to give a talk, but I didn't know how. The last three years of business records were gone. It was a bad situation, and I was upset in the dream."

Lee went on, "The next night I dreamed I was a teacher, part time at a local college. I was trying to find my classroom. Everyone gave me directions, but I couldn't find where I was supposed to be."

Lee finished with, "The third night I was in the hospital. There was a man there with his head bandaged up. He asked me to pray for him. I said okay. Then it hit me that I can do this! I remembered in this dream, the other two dreams. The man before me had cancer encapsulated but with 22 finger-like projections going into the surrounding tissue. I prayed over him. Then I saw him with a white thing on the bed next to him. It looked like jelly. The cancer had come out.

"Well?" He patiently waited for my reply.

I replied, "Oh my dear friend, it means you are doing exactly what God intended for you to do. As confusing as your life may have seemed to you, as many times as you tried to do other things in the earthly world and couldn't succeed, you were truly meant to be exactly what you became - A Man of God, a healer, a helper. You have accomplished what your original orders must have been!"

Sometimes in reaching out to help others, seeing them the way they are, we can see ourselves more clearly too. I wondered at the time, if his dreams were meant for me too.

DISCOVERING YOUR CALL

During one of our conversations together, Lee and I discussed how to know if you are in the right calling. This is the wisdom that came from his heart and mouth. He said, "Deb, a lot of times God nudges us to do little acts of love in other people's lives. Our responsibility is to be open and sensitive to hear God and do what we are told."

It makes sense to me.
How about you?

SECTION THREE
EVANGELIST, IVIE DENNIS

"STREET MINISTER"
"HELL SHRINKER"

Born: September 20, 1958, Lexington County,
         South Carolina

At 15 years old Ivie was a candy striper for Lexington County Medical Center. At 16 years old she graduated from high school in May of 1975. By the age of 17 she went to Holmes Bible Seminary for one year. At that time Ivie was the youngest state worker for South Carolina. She worked for the unemployment office. Over achieving seemed to be right up her alley!

By 18 she worked for Colonial Life Insurance as a claims auditor. Ivie married her first husband at the age of 19, and at 20, she miscarried a little boy, Thomas Scott. In 1980, she delivered a healthy baby boy David Lee. She delivered another healthy baby boy, Michael Ryan. Ivie was married for six years and lived in Germany with her husband in the military.

When she was 24 Ivie developed cancer for the first time and had a partial hysterectomy. She divorced her first husband while still living in Germany. In 1987 she remarried another military man, stateside, for six years. He brought her to Southern Indiana to live. Then they divorced.

Ivie met Ray Dennis in 1992, and they started dating. They were married in 1995 and stayed in Southern Indiana.

.

1998-2000 Berea University

2001 Ordained a Reverend

2001-2008 Street Ministry in Southern Indiana and Louisville, Kentucky.

2003   Surgery for colon cancer.

2008 Moved back to South Carolina to help her immediate family.

2010 Started working with the local hospice

2011 Diagnosed with Adenometastatic carcinoma.

July 11, 2011 The **fire of the Holy Spirit fell,** and she started immediately healing. All pain ended.

Evangelist Ivie Dennis is an ordained, non-denominational minister through Victory New Testament International, and is an End-time Handmaiden. She is an intercessor and a prophetess who ministers the Word of God with a powerful anointing. She moves and flows under the authority and direction of the Holy Spirit. Her passion is to raise up end-time handmaidens and extreme worshippers and to see the captives set free; the broken hearted sealed up by the Blood of the Lamb and to live the life of abundance as promised in God's Word.

She is a motivational speaker and has ministered at churches, prayer conferences and leadership seminars. She is the founder of Lifeline Outreach Ministries, Inc.

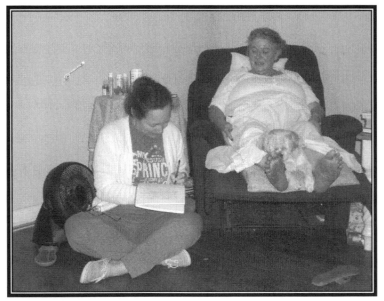

ABOVE: June of 2011 vacation trip turned mission trip. Ivie was still suffering from the effects of her cancer treatments.

BELOW: By the third day there, after group prayer Ivie was greatly improved and could move freely without suffering or weakness, as you can see!

HOW SHE CAME TO SERVE GOD

When Ivie was born, her mother, Eddie, prophesied when she heard Ivie's cry, "She cries with a demand, and many will hear the sound of her voice."

Ivie was born into a deep legacy of God. They were God-fearing people on her daddy's side, and her mother's Dad was a Baptist Minister. Ivie was raised in church. At 13 years old, she gave her life to the Lord. She was filled with the Holy Spirit with evidence of speaking in tongues! Ivie felt the call of ministry on her life at 14 and went to seminary for one year. Then, being young still, she "toyed" with the Lord. Ivie was not fully committed and available yet.

She went to work, got married, moved overseas and dabbled in the world's reality. She went astray and was far from God.

After her first bout of cancer, Ivie bargained with the Lord. It was then in 1984 in her hospital bed she vividly remembered seeing the Master - Jesus showed up at the end of her bed! Ivie felt something warm touch her ankle. She looked up and there was Jesus! He was radiant and his eyes were piercing! He was surrounded by kindness and love. It emanated from Him. So sweetly, **Jesus said, "Daughter, why do you run from me so?"**

Ivie replied very humbly, "I'm sorry I've run. I'm not promising I'll serve You right now, but what I'm promising You is I will serve You. I will be more radical for You than I ever was for the devil. I just want to see my kids grow up and be able to take care of them. Seeing grandchildren will be icing on the cake."

So softly, **He replied, "I love you."**
She replied back, "I love You too."

Immediately Ivie was restored. Her internal bleeding stopped, but a vein blew. Nurses ran in, and chaos commenced. "She's healed! How is this possible?" Color came back to her face, and she was healed. The cancer was gone, but to satisfy the doctor's, she had a partial hysterectomy.

In January of 1986 Ivie started getting her life in order to follow up on the promise she made to Jesus, which was to live her life for the Lord. But in 1992 she was still living her life in adultery - Ivie was living with Ray and they had not yet married. In June of 1995 she fell off a cliff and almost broke her back in half.

Ivie was in excruciating pain. The doctor's tried physical therapies, injections and medications. The Lord dealt with her during this time. He told her that she and Ray were to no longer live together unless they were married! Ivie went to Ray with the information the Lord had shared with her. His response was not as receptive as hers. Ray said he would not be pushed into anything. Ivie replied, "I'm not pushing you into anything. I won't live with you any longer. And if you don't want to get married, 'hit the road Jack'!" They got married one month later in October of 1995.

In 1996 Ivie lost her job, and they filed bankruptcy. They sold their home, and for a short period they were homeless. Then, Ivie had a vision in the Fall of 1998. Sight unseen, they were to buy a single wide and put it on land they would purchase. Shortly after moving in, God miraculously healed her back!

At a local Assembly of God Church in 1999, Ivie started a seven day fast. It was the first week of July. She sought out the Lord for direction. Ivie secluded herself and took a week off of work. There was no talking, and she went before the Lord on her face. Ivie wanted to hear the Lord's voice, and the Lord's voice she did hear! God spoke to her through visions, prophetic words, and she even saw Moses!

Everyday Ivie saw something different happen. She saw Moses in the field, so she marched around that field seven times. God allowed her to see Moses. He looked angelic. Moses was clad in a shepherd's clothes. By the third day of her fast, she was on the floor, prostrate before the Lord. The Lord took Ivie to her heritage. She saw her great-grandma Laura.

Laura was in a field crying. She was praying for all her children unto the 1,000[th] generation. This would have been in the 1870's to the 1880's. Laura was in a white dress with a rose colored print. Ivie saw her great grandmother during the time of a great drought. Laura prayed for rain to water their fields and feed their family and the people around them. She ended up feeding over 5,000 just like Jesus did!

Laura gave birth to 10 children, and they all served the Lord. Out of Ivie's grandmother Rosa, came over 40 ordained ministers, from great-grandmother's and grandmother's prayers.

Years later, Ivie's Grandma gave her a picture of her Mother in a rose colored print dress. Then she verified the very story that Ivie had witnessed in her vision.

At the end of the seven day fast Ivie was hungry for God's word! And God was hungry for her! God said, *"I want you to preach my word, but I don't want you to come under a denomination umbrella!"* He then told her He wanted her to go to school.

She asked, "Why school?"

And God said, *"Because I am going to send you to places where you will need credentials."*

True to His words, God led Ivie to Berea College where she graduated July 30, 2002. She was now a Reverend. Shortly after this, Ivie started Lifeline Outreach Ministry, "LOM".

Ivie ministered for eight years to the people in Southern Indiana and surrounding states. She fed the hungry, clothed the naked, visited the prisoners, healed the sick, counseled the poor in spirit and down hearted, did mission work, and had a huge successful food pantry and kitchen for many years.

I would know because my husband, Mark and I were on the Board of Directors of Lifeline Outreach Ministry for over two years. And, we were faithful volunteers every Monday and Tuesday at the Ministry to help process food brought in from the large food banks in the area for distribution.

MISSION TRIP
1500 SOULS

The summer before God called Ivie to start LOM, Lifeline Outreach Ministry, He put her on course for a mission trip to Mexico.

The first day of the mission trip to Mexico was in a park setting. There were idols and sun gods all around the worship team. Warrior shields up!

The passion for Jesus from the Mexican people lured them in. For six hours the team ministered to 1500 people, the largest group that showed up during the whole trip.

People were set free and crying out! What an amazing first day it was. And this was only the beginning!

ON THE THIRD DAY THE LAME WALKED

The third day the worship team was there, they were assigned to a shopping mall square. They presented a drama that was familiar to all in the region, The Passion of Christ.

After the play was over, a wheelchair bound man, weeping about all his losses was approached. They asked him, "What do you want from Jesus today?"

He replied, "I want to walk."

"Do you have enough faith to get up out of that chair?"

He had one simple answer, "Yes." He declared it.

Four of the ministers prayed together stirring up their own faith, then they reached out for him and the Holy Spirit fell! All around they smelled the fragrance of God. Pastor Ivie felt power go out of her hands to the man in the wheelchair.

The paraplegic raised up his arms and his legs! Then he put both feet on the ground, and jumped up praising God! He leapt about! He was delivered from 25 years in a wheelchair. It was instantaneous regeneration! One of the highest levels of miracles! Because of that great miracle, 100 souls came to the Lord and received Jesus.

RESURRECTION OF THE DEAD
THE FOURTH DAY

The worship team found themselves on the fourth day at ten in the morning, in a small remote village. They walked through the area passing out tracts and witnessing to anyone who would listen.

Suddenly, a woman came bolting out of her hut door screaming! The interpreter told them the baby in her arms was not breathing. The ten people on the team ran to her! The six week old infant was indeed blue and non-responsive.

The team members prayed in spirit and in tongues. They laid hands on the baby. They commanded the spirit of death to come out of that baby! They prophesied, "He will live and not die!"

Before their eyes, the infant boy took a breath, then another and another until his color was fully back, and he was responsive with a loud cry!

Everyone cried and they prophesied a great call over his life!

God showed up that day large and in charge and gave that baby his life back. They were sure he was rescued to be a mighty warrior.

The village people and the whole group saw an instant miracle. As they left the village, the word went forth before them just like the apostles of old.

THE GREAT FEAST

The last day of the mission trip in Mexico was a grueling one. Even the interpreter was worn out. It was between 115 degrees and 120 degrees Fahrenheit. There was no air conditioning. Pastor Ivie was suffering with edema (swelling) and was worn physically out.

The local pastor and his wife took her to their home. She slept in their bedroom that had an air conditioner. Ivie recounted how she could feel the presence of God in that room. Peace and joy seemed to come from the very walls themselves. She was able to go to church with them that evening.

At dinner, a long table was set up. Twelve to fifteen family members gathered around, and they prepared a feast! Authentic Mexican dishes were served, and Ivie's plate was the first one given out.

Before the meal began, they all laid hands on Pastor Ivie and prayed in Spanish. A young girl there who spoke some English told Ivie that she glowed. The glow filled the house! Simple kindness permeated the air. Then the meal began!

Ivie noted at the end of this story that the meal was spicy hot!

STEPPING OUT IN FAITH

Six years after Ray and Ivie's marriage had begun, Ivie got a calling to go into ministry full time. At the same time, her husband felt compelled to change his job as well. It was during this time Ivie saw a vision for LOM-Lifeline Outreach Ministry. In faith they both left their jobs the fall of 2001 and looked for a sign from God they were on the right path. Their confirmation came in a big way! October 25th, a $5,000.00 donation check came in the mail to get LOM started. They were overwhelmed! God had heard their cry!

Then in December, just before Christmas, they received another donation of $5,000.00! God certainly made a way where there was no way. It was very humbling and confirming all at the same time.

This was what Ivie needed to start the paperwork for a non-profit status. A year later LOM was ready to launch. The couple collected a board and looked for a building. The Lord told her to keep it simple. In November of 2001 they were approved as 501C3 status.

By the beginning of 2002 they had started a food bank and clothes closet at the local Baptist church in Corydon, Indiana. The church blessed LOM with a $100.00 a month rental of space. Immediately, the ministry flourished.

It had begun.

OUR INTRODUCTION TO
EVANGELIST REVEREND IVIE DENNIS

While on what I thought was going to be a vacation that turned into a mission trip, I found myself one afternoon sitting in a hospital room in South Carolina and watched nurses tend to my dear friend, Ivie Dennis. At the time she was conquering cancer for a third time. As Ivie slept quietly in her bed, the urge to write down how we met begged to be written from inside me . . .

It was February of 2003. Mark and I had friends who went to a local Baptist church. Sara had been telling me for the last six months that there was a new minister at their church who started a soup kitchen, a food pantry, and a clothes closet for the poor. I thought she must be a very good woman to do so much for the indigent.

Valentine's Day had rolled around, and we were asked to a married couple's dinner with their church. We said yes and thought it would be a fun evening. I dressed in a sparkly red shirt with a long black satin skirt.

That evening there were about 60 people in attendance. At one point during the introductions, I heard someone with a southern accent from behind me saying to me, "Why sister, we have on the same outfit!" I turned around and met Reverend Ivie Dennis and her husband Ray.

There she was in all her Godly glory, wearing the same outfit as me. Smiling a beautiful smile of peace, she introduced herself and her husband. Her hair and make-up were meticulously done. She glowed with joy and enthusiasm. I smiled. I knew right away she had a special spirit.

By the end of the evening, we agreed to meet for an assessment of her health and nutritional needs.

By the end of the year, Mark and I were on the Board of Directors for Lifeline Outreach Ministry. It appeared to me, we signed up for a life time friendship.

MEETING THE PEYRONS
TOLD IN IVIE'S OWN WORDS

As February approached, the idea of a Valentine's Day dinner at the church for married couples came to fruition. This is where we met Deb and Mark.

"We were blessed to have connections with the local Baptist church and were invited to their Valentine Banquet. What a blast that was! It was there, oh my goodness! I met the most precious individual who was the most powerful woman of God." Tears formed in her eyes. She went on to say, "I knew I had to be connected to her." Now openly crying she said, "Her name was Debbie Peyron. I felt so connected to Debbie. Her love and passion for the Lord was so intense. I admired her giving heart, and she inspired me! I had the same love for Miss Debbie Peyron as David had for Jonathan. And Jonathan had for David. The connection at that banquet was a connection that will take us to the banquet hall in the New Jerusalem. I am grateful for every moment we got to spend together. I am forever grateful for the day she walked into that hospital room in 2003 and brought me a sweet little gift and a refrigerator magnet.

I am grateful for every prayer that she and her husband have prayed for me. I am forever grateful God has established such a deep friendship and relationship. I am forever grateful for her tenacity. I am most humbled and honored to be mentioned in this book."

** *Ivie, I wouldn't think of writing it without you! - Author.*

BUILDING BY THE BROOK

As LOM outgrew the little Baptist church in 2003, Ivie went looking for another building in which to house her ministry. There was a little building by the brook that a man wanted to rent for $1800.00 a month. Now I have to admit here, I was a board member at that time, and I voted no to that much rent. Ivie pressed on. She told God in her spirit if LOM was going to have that building He was going to have to pay for it! She heard in the spirit right back, "Trust Me." I was out voted.

Ivie told all members of the board the money would come from God Almighty. The board members had fear and shock on their faces. "But Pastor Ivie," one of them said, "there is no money in the ministry account."

I reminded Ivie I was not walking in the same faith. But, Pastor continued to tell us the Lord would bring it from the North, the South, the East and the West. God would bring it into her hands. "Okay."

A week before LOM moved, a lady came in at dinner and brought Ivie eight $100.00 bills. We rejoiced and praised the Lord. An hour later, a man walked in with $300.00. Another one came in with $100.00! She went home that night and in the mail was a check for $769.00.

The board members, including myself, were blown away at all the miracle money that had come through. We all asked, "Pastor, how long will we stay here?"

She answered, "As long as God pays the rent."

Of course.

Three months later, LOM was looking for another building to rent.

All in God's timing.

THE LITTLE YELLOW HOUSE
HOME AWAY FROM HOME

Ivie and Ray went out looking again for somewhere to rent when they spied it. It was a beautiful little yellow house right in the middle of the area they needed to serve most. The rent was $400.00 a month, and that was easy enough to manage. September 12th they found it, talked with the owner and moved in completely by the end of the month!

The owners let them have the first three months free! Yes, that's a miracle too! Financial miracles can come in many kinds, shapes and sizes! All LOM had to do was renovate for anything special they needed to convert a kitchen into a food pantry.

God then showed Ivie the places to go for materials, paint and items. It was all donated by local community business owners.

They served their first meal October 1st.
What an on time God we serve!

BREAKING OF THE BREAD
MANNA FROM HEAVEN

By now, LOM had been in the little yellow house for four months. God was bringing in donations to the center that kept it afloat. Physical and material donations were coming en-mass but monetary donations were trickling in.

On the day of January 25th, 2004 it was cold, icy and rainy outside. The kitchen staff didn't think anyone would come in for a hot meal, much less to pick up anything. The lady cooking for them that day informed Ivie just before 11 am, knowing they were to open their doors for lunch at noon, that there was no bread in the house. Did she want to serve bread with the meal?

Ivie responded to her this way, "If we are serving bread today, God will have to bring it."

Ivie gathered all the volunteers together in the kitchen. They started praying for God to bring bread through the doors. There was $18.95 in the ministry account. There was no way that was going to buy bread for all the people that would show up throughout the day for a meal.

At 11:55 am, before they opened, there was a knock on the back door. A young man came in. The cook came running into Pastor Ivie's office shouting, "Pastor Ivie! Pastor Ivie! You've got to see this!" A man was holding five bags of bread with five loaves in each bag!

He stated, "I was at the store trying to figure out what I could donate today. I prayed. Then God told me to go buy bread. Go buy bread. I put in a few loaves. God told me that was not enough. I decided I would fill five bags with bread, as much as they would hold!"

That day, cold and rainy as it was the little center still fed 187 people. The cook fixed and gave out all but the ends of the bread. She then took those pieces and made bread pudding for the staff and volunteers of Lifeline Outreach Ministry.

Pastor Ivie told the young man, "You do not know what part of a miracle you have played. What time did the Lord speak to you?"

He replied, "It was right before 11 am. I had been wandering around the store trying to think of what to bring before then."

The board members and volunteers who were there that day had their faith increased from a bush to a tree.

God provided.

FEEDING ANGELS UNAWARES

In February of 2004, LOM served over 1200 hot meals and gave out 1400 boxes of food. They were closing up after a long day of service to God. The front porch light had not been turned off yet. They were almost ready to leave.

It was snowing hard. Ivie, the cook, another lady and man were still on the premises. A knock came to the front door and Ivie answered it. There stood a little old man and woman. They had gotten off the interstate and were lost. They were on their way from Ohio to Texas. They asked God to guide them to get help. Now I would like to note here that LOM was no where near the interstate. A person would have needed directions to find them.

Well, this little old couple was so happy to see smiling faces they said, "We are looking for help. We are on our way to Texas. We're lost and hungry and almost out of gas! Can you help us?" They appeared to be in their late 70's. They went on, "We asked God to show us where to go. We have no money to go to a restaurant or to put gas in our car."

Ivie and the volunteers invited them in. Well, it's February and the elderly couple were traveling from Ohio to Texas. Ivie's curiosity was up. She asked, "Why are you traveling in the middle of winter from Ohio to Texas?" They gave their reasons which will not be addressed here. Only suffice it to say it was reasonable to go.

Ivie and her crew made them plates to go, gave them blankets and took them to fill their gas tank up. Then they sent them on their way. Two days later an anonymous check came in the mail for $1,600.00. You cannot out give God!

SHOE BOXES

It was Christmas time, December of 2004. LOM decided to have a shoe box ministry for the poor children in the area. They had applied back in the fall for a grant from a large corporation. They hoped it would have been there before then, but as December rolled on, the money had not yet made its appearance.

The group looked to their bank account to buy hats, gloves, crayons, socks, pencils and small toys. There were at least 25 children they knew of that would be attending the December 24th Christmas Eve party. There was $140.00 to be spread out among the 25. Pastor Ivie said to wait. "Wait on God." December 20th there was nothing. Prayers went up. December 21st there was still nothing. Rats. I confess that I had a stomach ache over it all!

On December 22nd the dam broke! The angels came through! At 10 am a check for the promised $2,500.00 showed up! Dollar Tree, here they came! I was blessed to be there that day. "All hands on deck!" We wrapped packages as fast as we could!

Then there was another knock on the door. A local company donated a whole host of turkeys! Wow!! Cooks! Man your stations! LOM served 500 hot meals on Christmas Eve. We gave out 25 presents to the children of the area. The boxes were stuffed to the gills!

One of the recipients was an 18 year old young man. He stood there crying, holding the box tight in his hands. "Why are you crying?" we asked. He told us it was his only Christmas present.

God gave to LOM beyond our wildest dreams! This is what happens when the love of Jesus impacts humanity.

CLOSE ENCOUNTERS OF
THE GODLY KIND

Ivie Dennis is a visionary and a prophetess. Her visions are as clear as any I have ever had. She has just had a lot more of them. From what she has told me they seem to come in clusters. For example the year 1999 Ivie was called to three different fasts.

The first one was for a vision of what she should do and in which direction the Lord wanted her to go. That was her first seven day fast when Ivie had seen Moses on her property-to-be, when she was ordered to march around it and make it hers. Ivie took a gallon of oil and anointed every inch of that place!

On her last fast of that year, a 21 day fast, which was a pivotal moment in time for her, Ivie saw God from the back. She was behind a rock, and His shadow passed by. The Lord directed her to go to the river and sit on the bank and write. She was ordered to take her bible and look over the water. That was when God gave Ivie a vision for LOM, Lifeline Outreach Ministry.

In 2003 she dreamed of three tornadoes. Ivie was in her house with her family. One tornado was out in the field, one was over their heads, and one on the other side of the house that hit her in the back!

Interpretation: There was going to be a physical attack on her back area. Shortly, she was diagnosed with cancer of the colon causing pain in her lower back area.

In 2007, she dreamed and had visions again. This time it was of snakes. One bit her heal. That was the year she had her final hysterectomy with great suffering. Ivie also suffered many other hardships all through 2008.

The following prophetic word was taken directly from the writings of Ivie Dennis from the Holy Spirit on the morning of December 31, 2007.

I awoke with a vision of a very large golden gate sitting on a cloud and the gate was open with a flood of water coming out of it. The waters looked like that of Niagara Falls. I saw a great mist from the waters and the Holy Spirit spoke this interpretation to me.:

"Wake up my church, wake up! The floodgates are opening in 2008. The gates are open in 2008. Wake up church, wake up! The gates of 2008 will be the entrance way to new boundaries, new business plans and endeavors, new ministries, new frontiers, new relationships. The gates of 2008 will also be the exit from bondage and slavery of the things that are not pure. Wake up church, the dawning of a new day is here and the hour has come for Me to manifest Myself in a mighty and Holy way. There will be many trials and tribulations in this year of 2008, but I will manifest Myself in a greater way not known to any man of this generation. I have been sending my Word forth, and now I am going to show up in the midst of trials, in the midst of sorrow, and in the midst of chaotic situations. Wake up, and watch for the demonstration of my power. To those who have been faithful, I will reward and to those who have turned from me and their hearts are callous, I will bring judgment.

"The gates of 2008 are open, go through the gates, go through the gates. Take your place oh watchmen of the gates. Stand guard, keep watch, stay awake and alert.."

The Lord took me to the passage in Isaiah 62:10, "Go through the gates, go through the gates! Prepare the way for the people. Cast up, cast up the highway! Gather out the stones. Lift up a standard or ensign over and for the peoples."

Verse 11: Behold, the LORD has proclaimed to the end of the earth; Say to the Daughter of Zion, Behold, your salvation comes (in the person of the LORD), behold, His reward is with Him, and His work and recompense before Him...   And they shall call them the Holy People, the Redeemed of the LORD; and you shall be called "Sought Out, a City Not Forsaken."

The gates of 2008 have already been flung open.

"Trust **ME,** *let* **ME** *lead you through the gates and you will not despair or become down trodden."*

MOMMA EDDIE

Remarkable and miraculous occurrences happened during the years at Lifeline Outreach Ministry and the little yellow house on Water Street. The anointing was clear and present during all we touched and did, yet even this time was destined to come to a close.

God knew there was a coming storm over Ivie's family. She was soon to travel to South Carolina over and over where battles waited.

On December 31st 2007 Ivie was given a prophesy from the Lord. She saw a huge ministry plan for her with powerful victories. It was to come in little stages.

Every month there seemed to be a trial of some sort, one bigger than the next. In January, Ivie had gallbladder trouble. By February she ended up in the hospital. Thank God for Ray's insurance. Ivie had no sooner recuperated from that when there was a flood at their home. By April, 2008 was a weary year for her.

In May, she went to see her parents once again. Her Mother was in rapid physical decline. And by October when Ivie got the call that her mother had Histoplasmosis and was now legally blind in her left eye, Ivie knew she was destined to move back home to South Carolina. She called herself blessed to take care of her mother the last two months of her life.

Thanksgiving came and Ivie drove back to Indiana to be with her husband, Ray for the holiday. All seemed well.

Yet on November 29th, on her way back to South Carolina, the devil would once again attack the very life of Ivie Dennis.

It started out with pain and nausea. Ivie had reasoned possibly stomach flu on the horizon. But the closer she got to her destination, the worse it became. Unknown to her at the time, a one inch by one inch kidney stone blocked her left kidney duct and was rapidly turning the tables on her. Ray received an emergency phone call back in Indiana. Shortly after that, we got an emergency phone call. Ray said, "Deb, you and Mark have to take care of the dogs and the house. I'm leaving for South Carolina right now. It's Ivie. I think she's dying! Pray God doesn't take her!" It was the most scared I have heard a man's voice in all my life.

I hollered, "Mark, help! Ivie's dying! Pray with me quick! Ray is getting ready to fly to South Carolina now!"

Mark got back on the phone and told Ray he would take him to the airport right away! Mark assured Ray we would take care of everything back here at home. Did he need any money? Please God, don't let Ivie die! Don't let her die!!

Hours of prayer turned into two days of prayer. Another physical attack! The antibiotic the hospital put her on caused an allergic reaction so severe Ivie was almost unrecognizable. For a second time in as few days, her life was almost taken. Prayers went up non-stop.

By the dawn of December 5th Ivie was finally well enough to go home. As weak as she was, she knew she needed to go be with her parents. Ray stayed and nurtured all three family members, his wife, her mother and her father.

Finally the word came down from the Lord, "Ivie will live and not die."

A week later, December 17th, Ivie's Momma, Eddie woke up crying with pain. The family called an ambulance. She was admitted with Cellulitis, and on December 20th Eddie was diagnosed with Non-Alcoholic Cirrhosis of the Liver, advanced, and terminal.

On Christmas Eve Eddie spoke her last words to Ivie. She said, "I love you. Take care of your Dad." Christmas Day Ivie stayed with her mom and sang hymns and songs.

Early on December 26th, 2008 Eddie went home to be with the Lord forever.

HOSPICE

All of 2009 found Ivie trying to piece lives back together. The earthly rock of her families' foundation had gone to be with the Lord, and Ivie was left to help the family pick up all the pieces.

Clothes were donated. Personal items were given out between the children. And there was Dad, William, to take care of.

To add icing to the cake, Ivie's youngest son was in the middle of a messy divorce and custody battle for his four children. He needed his Momma more than ever.

"Fastest Year Ever" award went to 2009.
May it never come back around again!

Ivie noted in her journal in January of 2010, she had peace about the future. She got a job substitute teaching for the rest of the semester. Over the summer she looked for more work. *("Since I couldn't live on nothing, Deb!")*

That August she became a hospice certified nurses assistant. She was practically hired on the spot.

Who knew but God, where this road would take her?

A DOG'S TALE INTRODUCTION

We were still on our vacation turned mission trip. It had already been a hard morning. Pastor Ivie had awakened with an allergic reaction to the adhesive on her wound care. After a few very short phone calls, Ivie and I kissed the guys and the kids good by and off we went back to the hospital for a second day of emergency visits. I was learning to drive the new area very quickly.

We arrived at the hospital and got Ivie upstairs fast. The nurses came in and did their "angelic thing." Ivie received her infusion and instruction for care. After praying over the nurses, we headed back to the house.

As we arrived we met the rest of our crew coming out of the house. They were setting off on an adventure and would be back later. We again kissed all good-bye. Ivie and I came inside and found breakfast waiting for us. We ate and then went into the living room so she could be made comfortable. I settled down to write more God stories.

Ivie started the conversation with, "I know you want to hear my stories about visions and encounters, but I want to tell you about my dog."

"Excuse me, your dog?"

"Yes."

"Okay. I'm ready to write when you are ready to talk."

The word "hard" seemed to be in the middle of everything for Pastor Ivie for the last five years. She had surgery after surgery on her own body in various and diverse places. Her family in South Carolina had also needed her help. Ivie had a kidney stone that almost took her very life. Her own dear Mother passed away Christmas of 2008. She had been her best friend.

The marriage of her beloved son, DJ ended, and he needed help to raise four small children. And now, she had another bout with cancer, for a third time. How much more could a body or soul take?

But to her, it was no more than her new little dog had been through. Chloe, an eight year old Shih Tzu, by the time she had entered Ivie's life, "hard" was in the middle of everything the little dog had been through as well.

Just maybe, they were well suited to fit each other's needs.

A DOG'S TALE
BY REV. IVIE DENNIS

This excerpt is taken from "A Dog's Tale" by Pastor Ivie with her permission, with very little editing. – Author.

The first real experience I had with my very own dog was in May 2002. My husband and I were foster parents to a set of twin girls. Their grandfather brought a border collie mixed with chow puppy all the way from Houston, Texas to our home in Corydon, Indiana where we resided at the time. The grandpa assured us that the puppy would not grow too tall and did not chew up things. So, we agreed the puppy could stay. Needless to say, the puppy way outgrew our estimations and chewed up everything in sight! I was not a happy camper to put it mildly. I did everything I knew to break this puppy from chewing shy of choking her like a chicken!

My son, DJ, gave me a prophetic word concerning this puppy and I quote, "Mama, I believe God has sent this puppy to you to teach you how to love unconditionally. After all HE has called you to minister to the homeless, the poor, and the broken-hearted. What better way to teach you unconditional love than to train you with this puppy that is constantly chewing up your favorite shoes, clothing and Dad's cordless screwdrivers?" My son definitely had heard from the LORD on this. Over the next year this puppy who we named Brooklyn Renea, grew into a loving companion.

In May, 2003 I was diagnosed with cancer for the second time. My husband was working two jobs; first shift and third shift sleeping during the second shift. One night he had gone to work on his third shift job and I became extremely ill. I was throwing up violently and had gotten so weak I could barely hold my head up. I managed to pick the phone up and call my husband. When he answered the phone all I could say was "please help me." I dropped the phone onto the floor and lay on the bed crying. I felt so alone.

I prayed for God not to let me die in that bed all alone. All of a sudden, I sensed a presence of the Holy Spirit in my room so strong and the Peace of God just over flowed upon me. I felt a sensational strength rising up in me and as I rolled over on my side, there was Brooklyn with her head on the bed and her eyes very intent on me. It was as though she was speaking to me through those big beautiful brown eyes saying, "It's okay Mommy, you are not alone. I am here with you and I am watching over you."

I stroked her sweet beautiful head and was so comforted by her. I apologized to her for all the times I had spanked her for chewing up stuff. After all it was only stuff.

I asked her to forgive me in my ignorance and promised her from that day forward, I would never strike her again, and have not. I looked her square in the eyes and told her how much I loved her and thanked her for being my friend and companion. She stayed in that guarding position until my husband arrived home some thirty minutes later. During those 30 minutes, I did not get sick and knew that God had answered my prayers and would not let me die alone. He used this once "wild" little puppy to show me what unconditional love really was. After all the spankings she got and all the times I would scream at her and the time I picked her up and threw her out the back door and told her to leave and never come back, she still loved me unconditionally. And, for me that day was the day I learned to love her unconditionally.

Fast forward this story to the year 2011. Brooklyn is alive and well and still brings me such great joy. I consider her to be one of my dearest friends on this planet, and I shall never forget how God used her to minister to me in such a dark hour of my life. Since Brooklyn became a part of our family, we have gotten two other dogs from puppy to adulthood. They are Shih Tzu dogs. They are our babies and get along amazingly well with Brooklyn. However, there is another twist to this story. Because of circumstances beyond our control, my husband and I have had to live in two separate states since 2008. He is in Indiana, and I am in South Carolina. At any rate, I did not want my Ray to be all alone in Indiana so I left all three of the dogs with him. I was really missing my babies and began to pray for another Shih-Tzu. I did not want to have to pay for one because money was tight, and I believe in miracles even if it is for a free dog.

Again the Lord used my son, DJ to minister to me with a dog. He came home one evening in late August 2010 and said very excitedly, "Mama, I found something for your birthday that you have been wanting for some time, but I wanted to run it by you first before I get it." The first thing out of my mouth was, "You had better not gone and paid for a Shih Tzu puppy, because you know the money situation." He replied, "No, Mama, it is a free Shih Tzu, and she is eight years old. The people want to find a good home for her because they can't spend the time with her she needs." I was rejoicing and thanking God for bringing me a miracle dog...free!

On August 26, 2010 we drove over 100 miles to go and pick up my free dog God provided for me. Her name was Chloe. When we picked her up, she was so thin and frail. I could not believe what I was seeing. She smelled of an unfamiliar scent. The owners told us that she had just given Chloe a bath, but trust me, this was not the smell of a clean dog. The foul odor was so strong we had to ride home with the windows down to keep from becoming sick.

Over the next few months, this "free" dog cost me almost $1,000.00 in vet bills. The owner confessed to DJ that Chloe had been caged up for five years and had not seen a vet during that whole time. Chloe's anal glands were so impacted

139

that toxins were in her blood stream. She had a very serious skin infection, was in malnutrition and had an eye disease which would cause me to have her eyes removed on September 10, 2010.

She had been kicked in the mouth and had lost a couple of teeth. But in October 2010, I had to have all but two of her teeth removed because of infections in her gums. I was so hurt for this precious little animal, but also confused as to why God wanted me to have such a sickly dog. I did not question God's reasoning, but did ask Him to give me some understanding of it all. The Holy Spirit plainly spoke into my spirit these words, *"I knew you would nurture this wee dog back to life, and I will use her to nurture you back to life."* Wow! I thought. "Do you mean something is coming down the pike that is going to require me to be healed again Lord? Are you preparing me for another physical battle?" The answer came so quietly, *"Yes, dear one. Just don't be afraid and trust Me."*

As time has passed it is now July, 2011. Chloe is amazing. She knows exactly when I am in the house and can find her way around anywhere. She used her two little teeth to chew on small doggie bones and pig ears. She jumps up and down from my and her recliner when she wants me to hold her. She now weighs in at 14 pounds and is healthy as a horse. As for nurturing me back to life, I was diagnosed in April 2011 with a third bout of cancer. This time I would have to endure chemotherapy and radiation. In times past that was not an option. I had surgery in May 2011 to try to remove the mass in my back. The surgery was unsuccessful. Chemo and radiation were a must.

Six days after the surgery and home from the hospital only for three of those days, I landed back in the hospital with an illus which is a fancy medical term for bowel blockage.

140

I stayed another five days in the hospital, but had family members taking care of my Chloe. Upon my return from the hospital the second time, I was very weak and emotionally drained. God's loving words came back to me one afternoon while I was holding Chloe in my lap and loving on her. He reminded me of His promise that Chloe would nurture me back to life as I had done for her. On that day, I felt so loved not only by God, but by Chloe, and I knew He was using Chloe to nurture me back to life. I began to feel a strength rise up in me just as I had done back in 2003 with Brooklyn. I am getting stronger each day and even with the chemo and radiation, I am feeling wonderful. I have lots of time to hold Chloe and rejoice with her that God put us together.

I don't know if any of the readers of this story can relate to the power of animal therapy, but I believe God uses whatever we need to teach us, mold us and heal us. I am forever grateful for my loving companions Brooklyn, Boaz, Brandi Rhea and Chloe.

THE ROAD TO HOME

LEFT TO RIGHT: Deborah, Ivie and her son, DJ.

One of the first families Ivie went to help with hospice was an elderly gentleman. His family fell in love with Ivie. They unofficially adopted her. Ivie took care of their loved one until the very end. It was decided after the funeral, they were all to stay in touch.

She headed back to school that fall. We planned to go visit Ivie and her family that spring, but it seemed we had to wait our turn in between family emergencies.

By mid-April, Ivie's father, William had been diagnosed with Renal Failure. Ivie was due to see the same Nephrologist two days later. She had had bad pain too and feared kidney stones were back. An MRI on Good Friday revealed four stones, and on the 26th of April the real culprit was diagnosed. There was a large metastatic tumor wrapped around the nerves of her lower back. It was cancer.

But God orchestrated the right doctor at the right time. They immediately started chemotherapy and radiation. Finally days opened up for us to visit by the end of May. It coincided with the release of my first book. The delivery site for the first 25 books was to be at Ivie and DJ's rental home.

The first two of the four days I found myself taking Ivie to the hospital for emergency visits. Mark watched the children while her son had business meetings. Our vacation turned very quickly into a mission trip. It was all God's perfect timing. By the middle of the third day, we had all had it! Ivie's sister came over, DJ was home, and we gathered the children around. Ivie sat in the recliner pale and so weak she had trouble walking any distance.

We all prayed a round robin prayer, each one taking a turn after another. We didn't give up until she had victory! After 45 minutes of continuous prayer, the fire fell. Ivie jumped up out of her chair hollering, "Victory! Victory!" She went and grabbed her tambourine, and we all started clapping and cheering for the Lord.

By July 11th she finished her miraculous healing. All the pain was gone. Her healing had fully caught up with her. Things went very fast from then on. Ivie announced to her doctor that "Dr. Jesus has healed me, and I don't need anymore hospital treatments."

End of discussion.

July 15th – There was no more chemo.
July 20th – God spoke. *"Find land. You're moving."*
Ivie and her son looked through July. The right place had not presented itself yet. In August they contacted a realtor for help. Now they got somewhere!

It was five acres with a view of the mountains. It already had a beautiful large modular that was a twin to what

143

she had left behind in Indiana. With four bedrooms and two bathrooms, it was plenty big enough for her son and his family. Cash offer of $80,000.00 accepted. Glory to God!

This is where help from another source came in for this family. Friends blessed them with a private loan. "And by the way Ivie, would you like your own place on this land, too since we got such a tremendous deal on it?"

"Yes and yes!"

An equally beautiful small one bedroom modular was set up on their land on September 30, 2011, all for a small monthly fee. Was this the road to her next home?

The Journey to Eternity! Amen!

SECTION FOUR
JIM AND ANN CARTER

"LAY MINISTERS FOR THE LORD"

Jim Carter: Retired
Wife: Ann Carter
Born: April 15, 1942
Born Again: April 1971
Beginning of the Charismatic Movement
Tail end of the Jesus Movement in the late 1960's
Mission Field: Pastor, Teacher, Prophet, Speaker
Ordained: Under the articles of Ordination by a
          Baptist Minister
He walks in the Holy Spirit filled gifts of:
          Prophesy and Deliverance

Ann Carter: Retired
Husband: Jim Carter
Born: September 10, 1944
Born Again: Palm Sunday 1973
Mission Field: With her husband
She walks in the Holy Spirit filled gifts of:
          Deliverance and Prophesy

PRECIOUS GIFTS

So, I was at a TOPS meeting with my very best friend of 37 years, Vicki Sampson. She had asked me to give a talk at their weekly meeting about the Candida Diet. Vicki had thought maybe something a little different could help jump start their group on their progress toward lower weight and better health. I was happy to do it. I also felt compelled to bring seven copies of my new book called "Walking in the Supernatural." (Re-released in 2012 as "Miraculous Interventions.")

We arrived at the meeting on a dark and stormy night. Already half of the people who were to attend had cancelled. It was too bad a night! The facilitators of the group came in shortly after us. They were a very nice couple. He introduced himself and his wife as Jim and Ann Carter. At that time, I had no idea what God really had in store for us.

Jim stood up and called the meeting to order. They went over old and new business. He eventually got to the main speaker, me. Jim read a nice introduction, and I spoke for almost a half hour on diet and health impacts. I answered all the nutrition questions I could. Polite applause erupted at the end of the program.

Vicki stood up and announced that I had also written a book on miracles. She asked if anyone wanted to see them. Many people came forward and started asking questions wanting to buy one. Would I please sign and number them?

"Why sure!"

After class was over I was asked to join everyone for dinner at a local restaurant. I was delighted. Unknown to me at the time, Jim and Ann had already planned to buy my dinner.

Vicki and I joined the rest of the group at the local restaurant and had a lovely time! The food was good and the conversation was filled with fun and laughter!

While we were standing in line to pay bills, Jim and Ann started talking about a group of people back in the 70's and 80's that went around baptizing people in the Holy Spirit. It was the exact same group of people that had baptized my good friend, Lee Schwarz in the 1970's! Wow! Our phone numbers were exchanged, and plans were made for the Carters to come to our home and have dinner with Mark and myself. I was already looking forward to it.

THE FIRST SUPPER

Jim and Ann arrived at our home in Corydon, Indiana on a warm Saturday afternoon at the end of July. Mark welcomed them with heart felt handshakes and hugs. I had cooked all day making one of Mark's favorite meals in honor of their first supper with us.

These gentle people blessed us with home made gifts. How special. The hand made stained glass sun catcher was a beautiful color of teal in the shape of a dove descending, as if bringing blessings from the Lord above.

We sat and talked in our living room. We got to know a little about each other before dinner. I also asked if I could bring out my tape recorder and pen and paper to take notes on some of their amazing stories on their walk with the Lord.

They said, "Sure."

So began their stories . . .

ROUGH STARTS

Both the Carters had rough starts in this world. Extreme abuse was heaped on both of them as children. How either one of them lived through it was a miracle in and of itself!

Jim's Dad was a hard drinker. Hard drinkers usually make hard parents. He was hard to be around and physically abusive. Even harder to work with when Jim got older and wanted to buy the family business. Because of his upbringing, before the Lord got a hold of him, Jim made a hard husband too. He carried a lot of anger and fear with him.

But, that was all Ann knew growing up, she thought this was a normal life for her, even though in her heart, she ached for normalcy. Ann had been molested by her step-father at the age of seven years. That incident colored everything she went through for a very long time. Of course, the perpetrator made her feel as if it was her fault. This guilt went deep into her heart and soul. She couldn't tell her mother. Ann was sure her mother would blame her too. After all, she had beaten her enough as it was. Ann didn't need one more thing to be sorry for. Her mother had been certifiably insane since Ann could remember. Ann's mother had had over 135 shock treatments. Nothing helped. Hell was hell for all of them, and that was it.

How do you start a life together with that much turmoil? How do you heal bouncing off physical and emotional pain and suffering that went to their very bones?

Why, nothing short of the blood of Jesus could heal this.

JIM'S STORY

Jim had a hard upbringing that colored his first 20 plus years of vision. He thought, reacted and loved all the wrong ways. His understanding of truth was all wrong.

But under the power of the Holy Spirit, Jim's soul cried out to know God and understand Him and to have understanding of all that he had been through. He ached to be the man God called him to be, but he didn't know how or even where to start.

That was when he got involved in the "Jesus Movement" in April of 1970. At a Billy Graham Crusade, Jim received Jesus as Lord and Savior. Immediately Jesus started working on him. Jesus called Jim to a deeper walk. Jim went back for awhile to the church of his youth, Catholicism. Then God sent a "Holiness" man to answer some of his many questions.

One afternoon while seeking the face of God for help, Jim went and sat in his van and requested the Holy Spirit come. And come He did! Power and light struck Jim! His spirit lifted. Jim threw a fleece to the Lord God. He asked God to heal his Dad and to do several other things. If God would do this, Jim would take it as a sign he was to teach CCD classes.

Jim got out of the van and his phone rang. Literally, he got everything he asked for in an instant! Wow! Yes, he kept his word and taught CCD classes for several years. He became part of the Catholic Charismatic Movement in 1972. They would go under the spirit and praise God and sing until 1:30 in the morning!

The next April as Jim was watching the "Ten Commandments" movie. He realized, "That's my God! He can do anything!" His real journey had just begun. By two a.m. that morning, Ann woke Jim. She had fallen under conviction that very evening and ask Jim to pray with her to receive Jesus as her Lord and Savior. She was now so in love with Jesus!

Jim started singing with the choir of the celebrated Evangelist Katherine Kulhman. She would fall under the Holy Spirit while preaching, point to a whole group of people and they would all fall out in the spirit. Miracles would happen left and right on the stage. It was as if the Holy Spirit was sizzling on that very stage!

But there was still more to come!

Ann and Jim Carter with Deborah in the kitchen of the Carter home . . .

. . . and Mark with Ann and Jim Carter.

NOTRE DAME

By the early to mid-1970's, the Catholic Charismatic community at Notre Dame was holding conferences of the Holy Spirit. One of them was led by "The Fabulous Five". These were five protestant ministers who walked in the power of the Holy Spirit. Their mission was to teach Catholic clergy and lay people about being born again, or Charismatic's - same gifts with different names. Jim and Ann, the pastors, and their entire group went up to Notre Dame in South Bend, Indiana in a big, chartered bus.

Along the way back from South Bend, they were approached by 70 nuns also on the way back from the Notre Dame conference. The nuns asked them how they could be saved, too! They wanted to be baptized in the Holy Spirit.

From South Bend to Indianapolis, they all traveled together. And one by one, the nuns were all baptized in the Holy Spirit. The Spirit was prevalent on the bus with them. The ministers preached what God did for us when he raised Jesus from the dead!

When Jesus died and rose, the veil was torn. We as Christians, as brothers in Christ Jesus, can now boldly come before the throne of God.

Every nun received her own prayer language*.

* This is the gift of "Speaking in Tongues" as in Acts 2:3-4, "And there appeared unto them cloven tongues like as of fire, and it sat upon each of them. And they were all filled with the Holy Ghost, and began to speak with other tongues, as the Spirit gave them utterance."

MORE OF JIM'S STORY

By 1976, Jim still wanted to learn more of the Bible. During this time, he met a very learned Baptist Minister. The minister told Jim he had to ask his priest if he could teach him in bible studies. Jim approached his priest and asked him if he could take bible lessons from this man. To his joyous surprise the priest gave his okay.

Jim was submersion baptized later that same year. After that, he felt God speak to him. God said, **"Go now."**

Jim started a home church ministry. Jim and his wife Ann have traveled all over America joining revivals, prayer groups, teaching the gospel of Jesus and consider themselves street evangelists. They hold devotions every night, praying together with power and authority.

ANN'S STORY

Living with guilt and shame for most of one's life can be exhausting at best. Ann knew she loved God with all her heart. Because of what she had been through, she could not see how God could love her back. She felt so unworthy. Ann wondered how she would ever get over all that had happened to her.

One night at her church, a man received a word of knowledge for her. He asked a question, "Is there someone out here who was hurt traumatically when they were young?"

Ann went forward. He prayed. He sought God's counsel and said to her, "Something happened to you at almost seven years of age. It has affected your whole life." At that moment Ann was thrown to the floor by the power of the Holy Spirit! She was not hurt. The man prayed over her and led her to delivery from this spirit of oppression.

She was healed that very night! It no longer had a hold on her. She was delivered and able to forgive all the people who had ever wronged her.

SOUND DOCTRINE

Jim and Ann have, through prayer and bible study, reached some wonderful truths that are very helpful in their lives, mine and maybe yours too.

"It is not the person, but the amount of Holy Spirit gifts inside the person that administers healing or accepts the healing. Yes, you need to be open to the Holy Spirit to be able to accept your healing. "

"God will use anything to save people!"

"Salvation is a free gift from God."

"Nothing can separate us from the love of God."

"The Holy Spirit is a gentleman. He will not enter into you or your situation unless asked or wanted."

"You cannot clean yourself up to be made presentable to the Lord. That thinking is backward. The Lord cleans you up. How? He does this by the 'pricking of your spirit' when you sin."

THE TROUBLE WITH RELIGION`
Jim's Teaching

When you are taught that you are only old sinners saved by grace and you must remain humble, the unworthiness that sometimes accompanies this thought, that you stay as "filthy rags", can keep you from a full indwelling of the Holy Spirit. This spirit of unworthiness can keep it from you.

Religion gets us to clean up the outside of ourselves. But on the inside, we are as dry bones. We are still holding onto the old man. We still feel guilty of the old things that have passed away! No more dry bones!

God is all about relationship building. That is why He sent His Son, Jesus. Jesus showed us in His words and actions how to talk with God as a *Father*, how to go before the Lord for help in any situation, how to handle everything from prayer to praise to thanksgiving. Jesus *died* and *rose* to bring us salvation. He keeps us from sin, death and hell. But He *lived* to show us the way to live and to have life abundant and to the full!

Don't you want that too?
I know I do.

BELIEVING ABOVE ALL ELSE

In the 1970's, while Jim and Ann were just getting into their stride with prayer and miracles, they were at a church gathering with about 30 other people. It was for praise and worship, then a meal together.

Well, one of the families present at the meeting had a small child who went to reach up on the table for some food. The problem was it was a very hot dish. And she knocked it over onto herself before anyone could stop her.

In an instant the little girl was scalded with second degree burns over most portions of her body. It all seemed to happen at once. The baby was screaming, everyone was screaming! But the Holy Spirit was with them. The parents grabbed the toddler up, and everyone surrounded them with strong prayers of healing.

Within a few minutes the child calmed down, the blisters went down, and the red skin faded to pink. Then she wiggled out of her Mother's arms and went back to playing.

I love the stories that end with "and they all lived happily ever after."
Bless God.

JIM'S PROPHESY

One of the last questions I asked before Jim led prayer over my husband and me was what he sees for the church and man's future. The man got quiet and went searching for God's reply, not his.

"The true holy ghost revival is still to come. It will be an agape flood."

Jim paused again to help us understand an example of what he had just prophesied. "There will be more door to door outreaches to find and help the lost. This will bring salvation and what that means to each and every person."

Jim and Ann have devotions every night. They pray with power and authority as the bible teaches us all to do. It is a real force to be reckoned with. Nightly, they become one with the Lord. Jesus is truly among them. He hears their every cry, word of praise, and thanks giving.

JIM'S WORD OF KNOWLEDGE
FOR ME

He said, "Deborah, pray for personal wisdom for any decisions you need to make and understanding for them. This way it takes the pressure off of you and Mark. You know God is making the decision for you, His best and highest will. Also, be in an attitude of prayer all your days. Be in active communication with the Father always. Talk with Him through out the day. In this way, Words of Knowledge will happen."

ANN'S PROPHESY FOR ME

These were words from Ann that touched my heart dearly. Even though they were meant for my ears only, I felt compelled to share them with my readers.

"God has put us *[Mark and I]* together. I am worthy in His sight. I am your sister in the Lord. *[Ann is my sister]* We are Jesus' friends.

"Don't tell your husband to leave you!" *[Spirit of unworthiness because of what I went through when I lost my job/business at the end of 2007]*

"Jesus died for all that come to Him! The body of Christ should be good to each other. We should reach out when in need and minister to each other. Remember these things I have taught you."

You bet. Thanks!

Jim and Ann Carter
are available for healing prayer.

Their address is:

2218 Stonehurst Drive
Louisville, KY 40242
Phone is 502-426-8536

SECTION FIVE
PRAYING FOR A FLORIDA CRACKER

LARRY AND MARILYNN CROSIER
LAY MINISTERS FOR CHRIST

Larry Crosier
Born: October 10, 1955
Born again: March 30, 1980
Walks in the office of a prophet
Angelic sightings and visions

Marilynn Crosier
Born: October 2, 1954
Born again: 1981
Walks in the office of Intercessory Prayer Warrior
Also a prophetess with angelic sightings and visions

They were told at the beginning of their mission field, if they were willing and obedient they would eat off the fat of the land. They were to pray and obey.

INTRODUCTION

Their story is one of a close walk with the Lord. Mark had grown up with Larry. They went to school together and knew each other's families. While Larry was born again early in life and trusting the Lord, Mark on the other hand did not decide to follow the Lord until his late 30's. For this and other reasons, they did not stay in touch until my first book; "Miraculous Interventions" was published. Larry and Marilynn heard about it, bought and read it, and then Larry went to find Mark. His wife wanted to meet the lady that wrote that book! Mark called me and told me they had invited us for dinner. Larry's wife wanted to meet me.

Larry and Marilynn Crosier
20th Anniversary

A FLORIDA CRACKER

Shortly after Larry was born again in the Holy Spirit, he started praying for a wife. He wanted a wife with the same heart for Jesus that he had. At 24 years old he started praying and praying. Larry prayed for a year and a half. He even enlisted help! A sweet, elderly lady at his church made it her mission to pray and listen for God's help with this matter too.

I should note here that Larry has always lived in Southern Indiana.

Almost a year and a half later, a very nice young lady from Florida had just started praying for God to send her a husband. Well, unknown to the both of them, they each had mutual friends who knew them both. God spoke to these friends, "**Put these two together**".

Larry wrote Marilynn a five page letter only knowing her name and that she was a Christian. He poured his heart out.

When Marilynn received his letter after only a few days of asking God for a husband, she had to pause to reply to this letter. This was important. She knew this would mean the difference in the rest of her life. It took Marilynn three weeks to put together everything she wanted to tell him too. When Larry received the letter he knew it was from his future wife. As soon as his eyes could finish reading the words on the pages, he called her and they talked for over two hours.

Yes indeed, this surely had to be a God intervention.

They wrote back and forth, sent tapes and went to meet each other's families. Within seven short months, they trusted God and each other and wed May 15th, 1982. They trusted God then to put them together, and they trust God now.

But this is just the beginning of their journey together.

HOME SWEET HOME

They were married on the wedding anniversary of Marilynn's parents, May 15th. Marilynn's father had passed away when she was only eight years old. What a tribute to her parents this was!

As with all decisions they made, they conferred with God. They had been married a few years when it made perfect sense to them to put out a fleece, for almost a year, for their first home. It took another woman from their church that saw it in a dream to come and tell them. God told them the specific amount they would pay for it.

They were very happy to have their new little log home. They thought they were set.

They wondered at the time what God would have them do next.

SPIRITUAL   WARFARE

Coming up on their tenth anniversary, still in their beautiful log home, there was trouble. There was infiltration. One evening Larry had had it. Early in the morning hours he wrote his wife a letter asking her what was wrong. Please explain why she didn't want him anymore. Why would she not be intimate with him?

Marilynn knew she had a problem. She was not sure when it had begun or where it started, but she knew it wasn't right. She couldn't be with her husband anymore. This caused trouble. She knew the signs. Who is the father of trouble? And what demon had raised its ugly head from inside her?

Larry came down with the letter. In Marilynn's spirit she knew it was time to do battle! She cried out for her husband to pray for her. She prayed for the name of the demon causing her trouble. As they prayed together, supernatural wisdom fell down upon them and named it "emotional instability." Now they could fight!

As they fought together in prayer, Marilynn felt the demon in her body. It had talons attached deep within her stomach. They cried out to the Lord for her release from this entity!

Then she felt her spiritual body rise up! Marilynn sensed it from her head to her toes! She coughed, and it came out. The smell in the room was of sulfur.

Release! Freedom!

Larry said, "Did you smell that?!"

"Yes!" She was now singing in joy, "Father of light shine down on me!" Harmony was back. Thank you Jesus! And that demon has never been back since. It has no home anymore.

SEASON OF HEALING

Shaking off the root of instability opened Marilynn up to be able to have more discernment in the spiritual realms. Now she could help other people fight battles, too.

There was a man they knew that had a hurt shoulder. Marilynn could feel his pain. It was excruciating. She started praying for him to be released from this. Instantly the pain left her, and him.

When people found out about Marilynn's "gifts" from the Lord, they called her for help. People with cancer and emotional pain were healed. Two people with hearing loss, when she touched them in prayer, it left them and they could hear normally again!

With emotional pain, she felt it as well. Marilynn is an empath. However, when she started to really feel people's problems, it scared her, and she stopped for a while. She felt she had to get a better understanding of what she was doing to go on with it.

A DOUBLE PORTION

The Crosiers know their bible. They understand when they pray for people and for themselves. So when Marilynn asked for a double portion, she knew exactly what she asked for. Just like Elisha in the Old Testament, she got it.

One night after they were both asleep around one in the morning, she became "drunk in the spirit." The Lord showed Marilynn her life. She watched it pass before her and He told her, "**All will be alright.**"

Marilynn smelled cookies, flowers and roses. She felt a heavenly angel coming up the stairs. She then heard the wings against the walls of the stair steps. As it entered the room she heard the clapping of wings together. She could see vapors in the form of a man. The angel walked to the end of their bed. She could feel the power of God was with him. He walked to her side of the bed and she started shaking in the flesh. It was the Holy Spirit of the living God!

He said to her, "**Our God is an all consuming fire.**"

When he left she asked the Lord what that was. What did it mean?

At the time there was no answer.

THE RIVER OF LIFE

The next night the anointing was still with Marilynn. When she went to sleep that night, she had a vision dream.

Marilynn saw what looked like a big Imax screen. And she heard a voice say, **"This is what Heaven is like."**

As Marilynn watched the screen she saw what looked like a glass crystal river. She knew it was the river of life. It ran all the way up to the throne of God. It was vibrant with colors she had never seen before. She could see the tree with the fruit of the nations on it. There was white gold in Heaven. Not at all like our earthly yellow gold.

The joy was so strong in the presence of the Lord. She heard, **"You can live like this."**

Then she was back in the flesh.

INTERCESSOR

By now Larry and Marilynn had been married over ten years. They had so much love to give. They wanted children, and lots of them.

One evening as she was again praying for the gift of children, the bed began to shake. Larry heard in his spirit, **"This is me. Don't be afraid."** The Lord told Marilynn she would be an intercessor for people. She would give birth in the spirit. He took away her desire for children. **"You are called to be an intercessor."**

She still is.

ORDERS   LUKE 4: 18-19

An "intercessor".

Marilynn asked for confirmation of this word. She got it. All night long the Holy Spirit gave her revelation. He spoke inside her and told her "**I have anointed you to preach the gospel to the poor, heal the broken hearted, preach deliverance to the captive, recovery of sight to the blind, set at liberty them that are bruised, and preach the acceptable year of the Lord!**"

She again asked for confirmation. It came to her in the form of two dreams.

Marilynn was in a cave. She could smell sulfur and feel evil. She saw an ape-man guarding Christian prisoners. Marilynn could see herself trying to get them out! The Lord gave her strength and she flew them out of there!

Another spirit dream came. Marilynn was again in a cave. People were being held captive by a gorilla. She snuck in to get them out and deliver them. They flew out one at a time. She saw evil spears with fire on them. It was cold, but she set the captives free.

Then, one evening at a women's seminar, a woman evangelist sitting at the same table as Marilynn looked her in the eyes and said, "You are going to be just like me." She quoted the same scripture that had been in her dream.
Marilynn asked her, "What about Larry?!
She replied, "He will be your helper."

MOVE

One day, in Marilynn's heart and mind, she felt God speak to her to move. He wanted them to sell their house, quit their jobs and move.

She did not question Him when this word came down. All she said was, "When, Lord?"

He replied, "**Three and a half months**."

Marylinn asked again, "Where to Lord?"

"Jasper, Indiana."

"Okay Lord but You have to tell Larry."

His reply was, "**I have already told him!**"

That night when Larry came home from work, he too had a word from the Lord confirming what she had been told.

In their minds and hearts, as they sold their first home, they envisioned what their new place would be like, even what it would cost. They put their petitions up to the Lord.

They got everything they wanted. The type of home it was, the land, the stocked fishing pond, even the amount of rent! A very nice Catholic family owned it and just wanted someone good to live there. It seemed God answered both of their prayers together.

The Crosiers told God everything they wanted and He delivered it all to them.

Tell God what you want.
Watch Him deliver it to you too in His own time.

A DREAM COME TRUE

The next day after the Lord had told them to move, Larry handed in his two week resignation from his excellent paying job. They put a sign in the yard to sell their home. God sold it in two weeks! Then they drove to Ferdinand and looked for a home.

They knew in the spirit they would be renting because they would only be there a few short years. In fact, it was only two years. As in the other story, the Crosiers put down on paper what they wanted from the Lord. When they saw it in the local paper, they knew they had to go see the property.

There it was! They pulled up to the driveway and knew this was it. It truly was everything they had asked for. A big pond was stocked full of fish, a two car garage, hardwood floors, everything. A large Catholic family blessed them with rent of only $200.00 a month for the next two years.

Now, the reason God had them move was to help a struggling non-denominational church down in that region. Later it became a Christian Center. You see, they were sent out to the mission field. The Crosiers were in training on how to be obedient. Just how far could they trust God?

All the way.

During this time they traveled with an evangelist for 18 months who was a prophet and a teacher. They were prayer warriors for him. They all prayed together before every service. Marilynn was a full gospel businessman's praise and worship leader for the Jasper chapter.

God brought Larry two different jobs. Marilynn was sent to work for Abbey Press.

Then, it was time to move again.

A GLIMPSE OF WHAT IS TO COME

In 1991, Marilynn saw a vision of many concentration camps. The people were destitute. They were physically and spiritually destitute. She was ministering to them.

[I ask the readers now, how close are we to this day]?

Marilynn also dreamed of houses destroyed. No food in the stores. She felt a premonition of great hurricanes coming to this land and massive tornadoes striking.

In a dream she saw an orphanage with no one helping the children. She was feeding them milk. The babies got all better. As Marilynn fed them more and more, she saw herself ministering to them.

A word of knowledge was given to her. **"And I will show thee things which thou knowest not."**

God showed Larry the earthquake in Japan of 2011. The day it happened he saw it in a vision while he was out mowing their grass!

As of this writing, this one is yet to come:

In 2008, this dream came twice two weeks apart. She saw a warehouse. People were working in it. She saw combat planes coming. It would be an attack. She saw men in fatigues with guns pointed. People were being captured.

LOOKING FOR THE PINE TREE

In 1993 they were to move back to Elizabeth Indiana. God again showed Marilynn where they were moving. She saw a vision of a pine tree in the front yard with a brick ranch home. Larry and Marilynn went to church that weekend at Grace Tabernacle. A lady at the church told Marilynn to consider going by a certain house.

When they went by that afternoon they knew that was it. They were home once again. It was exactly what she had seen.

They started out renting it for two years until 1995. Then, Larry's mother bought the home, and they rented it from her until she was ready to move in, in 1996.

As the time drew close for Larry's mother to move in and for them to move out, they started looking for land. After all, they had to live somewhere.

LOOKING FOR LAND

Land was so high! They looked everywhere high and low, and all they could find was high land! Finally, in desperation, Larry asked their pastor's father to sell them a plot off of his land. He asked for two acres, however, he refused to sell them land. Why? He refused because he wanted to bless them and *give* them land.

Wow! This kind of restores your faith in people.

The Crosiers proceeded to buy five more acres from him. Blessings came from both sides. They went to look for a modular to put on their property. Larry figured they could dig and pour a basement beneath it for bad weather. The Crosiers must have looked at hundreds. They prayed over and over, "Show us!" They prayed and looked until they were exhausted.

On their last trip out, they found one on sale, a close out model for $38,000.00. It had everything they wanted.

And, it was made in America. God sent exactly the right person to build their basement for 1/3 the cost.

God knows our means.

DRY SPELL

From 1997 until 2008, for almost ten years, they felt they were put on a shelf to mature and grow in knowledge, and they did.

It was then that Marilynn went to school for Cosmetology. She was so good at it that she became an instructor for five years. Larry's job went so well that he kept moving up to better paying jobs.

God was blessing them with provisional blessings to store up.

It was during this time that the Lord brought back to Marilynn the gift of intercessory prayer.

In 2009, the Lord showed her to pray "the Blood of Jesus" for protection over them. To pray to be surrounded by angels bringing divine protection.

Yes sir.

Larry and Marilynn Crosier May 2012

SHOW ME THE NEXT STEP
MORE PROPHESY

It was in the fall of 2011 that our families got to meet one another. During this time Marilynn began to have prophetic dreams. She felt we were an instigator in this activity. Doors were once again opening up for her.

Deborah with Larry and Marilynn Crosier in their Laconia home.

Mark with Marilynn and Larry Crosier

Marilynn dreamed she told her pastor to honor one of the elderly ladies in the church for all the years of her service. To honor her, Marilynn was singing "Oh Holy Night." Then she heard angels joining in. Marilynn could see the woman's husband who had died two years before singing with the angels.

The heavens themselves were honoring her.

SECTION SIX
FATHER MICHAEL OLSEN

"St Columba of IONA COMMUNITY CHURCH"

Occupation: Anglican Priest and Monk
Wife: Patricia Olsen
Married 24 years as of 2012

Sometimes in the process of interviewing people for their miracle stories, they realize they really do have an interesting story to tell and decide to write it themselves. That is what happened as I interviewed this couple.

Where did that leave our stories together? We agreed I would write an introduction to them for this book. I would also write the story of how we met and our stories together. The story of their past would be their book.*

" Deal."

I also informed them that I gladly gave them permission to use "our stories" together written from their perspective. This, in retrospect, made my job a lot easier.

I thought it would be of good interest at this point to tell you how we all met.

At the time of this printing we are seriously considering working together on their book project.

COINCIDENCE ON TOP OF COINCIDENCE

I've taught a couple of times over the years at TOPS, "Taking Off Pounds Sensibly". My best friend of 38 + years, Vicki Sampson, had asked me to come and teach a class so that everyone would have all the information they would need to eat healthy the rest of their life.

I could do that.

The day she picked was a day that Mark and I had off together. Wonderful! He could help me giving out papers and fielding questions. In the 10 years of my teaching and being in the wellness field, Mark had never come along to help. But he was happy to do it.

We arrived in Louisville early and spent some quality time with Vicki before class. The regular group showed up that evening along with a new couple, a husband and wife.

Between my talk and questions afterward, the meeting went a little longer than normal. Thankfully, the interest was high, and no one complained. The meeting adjourned shortly after 8:30 pm, and we prepared to leave when I was approached by the new couple.

The man initiated the conversation, "Hello, I'm Father Mike Olsen. You are charismatic." He stated it as if I had been preaching a half hour on the Holy Spirit!

I shook my head, stared at him with confusion planted squarely on my face and said, "How did you know that?"

Quite simply he replied, "The Holy Spirit told me."

I responded quickly, "That makes you my brother!"

With a big smile he said, "And that makes you my sister!"

He then introduced his wife to me, and I hollered for Mark to come over and meet these people! "Mark honey! Come quick! The Lord has set up another meeting for us!"

We introduced our spouses. Father Mike went on with the conversation, "The Lord wants us to get together. How can I contact you?"

I gave him one of my business cards with the book Miraculous Interventions on it. He looked at it and said, "Wow. You write books about miracles? We believe in all that too! We see "angel orbs", God's gold and miracles in our church." He smiled.

It didn't take me but a second to say, "We're coming to your church, and I'll write a whole chapter about you all!"

I gave him a copy of my first book, "Miraculous Interventions".

On the way home Mark and I spoke of how amazed we were at how God used the ordinary to bring together the extraordinary and we wondered where this path would lead us.

Fr Mike Olsen at a gathering May, 2012 in Louisville, KY

HELP   A   BROTHER   OUT

We met this fine couple ten days prior to going on a family vacation to Walt Disney World. Two days after meeting them, I received an e-mail from Father Mike. The Holy Spirit had told him to tell me their whole story in one e-mail.

Mike had lost his job nine months ago. The Olsen's were struggling. They too were going to Florida but not on vacation. Patti's father had died. They had little to no resources to get there.

I printed out their message and laid it on the kitchen table to show to Mark when he got home from work. When he got home and read the e-mail, Mark had the same reaction as me. He said, "I've got $50.00. What have you got?"

I replied, "I've got $50.00 too."

Then Mark said, "What have we got in the way of supplies that we could send with them on the road?"

We went into the back bedroom to check our vacation supplies. There was much more there than the eight of us could use on the whole trip. We set aside an almost full case of bottled waters, boxes of crackers, chips, chocolates and other various snacks to take to our newest set of friends. Evidently they needed us.

A few days later I took their supplies to their home. They were very grateful that two strangers would take their situation to our hearts. After we had chatted a few minutes, Father Mike started a very interesting conversation. He asked me, "Have you ever heard of or seen angelic orbs?"

I had some understanding of what he was talking about and said as much. He asked, "Would you be interested in seeing some pictures of them?"

"You have pictures? Yes! I would love to see them!"

I was all eyes and ears. He had a whole album of them. They were taken with different cameras, different situations and times, various places. It was almost as if they had been with him all of his life.

I asked, "Have you got any objection to being in a book about miracles?"

He laughed and said, "That would be fine!"

We knew our families would see each other again after our trips to Florida.

We wished each other well on our separate journeys, and promised when we came back, we would come to their church to see what it was all about.

At that time, we had no idea of the miraculous journey we were about to embark on. The greatest days, it seemed, were just ahead of us.

JANUARY 1, 2012 - INTRODUCTION

After the best family vacation ever, time seemed to fly by between Halloween and Christmas. The end of 2011 was busier than normal for us. We were used to Mark's hours ramping up to 70 hours a week, but it was our first time to see me have a busy Christmas season as well.

"Christmas Chaos" hit the stores just days before the Thanksgiving weekend. I felt like half the season was already gone! I made many appointments for book signings, school Christmas parties, church teas, radio station interviews and book deliveries to local Kentucky and Indiana book stores.

Our home church shuts down during the holidays so people, including our pastor and his wife could travel to see their families. Every time Mark and I had a free moment, off we flew to the department store for another person that had been inadvertently left off the "good" list.

During this season we did make time to get together for dinner with Larry and Marilynn Crosier. At the end of our evening together, we checked our schedules to see when we could get together again. Our new friendship was off to a very nice start. Larry said, "Deb, the first day I have open is Sunday January 1, 2012."

I replied, "Okay. Hey, do you all want to go with us to the new church over in Louisville? It's the one where the priest is seeing angels and God's gold."

Larry and Marilynn grinned at each other. He said, "That sounds like a plan to me!" I called St. Columba and asked Fr. Mike if that was a good date for us to come by. He said that would be a great date because their Christmas party was to be after the mass. We could stay and fellowship.

Wonderful! We agreed to bring a side dish. I called Marilynn to inform her, and all was set.

TOP: Larry and Marilynn Crosier
BOTTOM: Mark, Deborah and Fr Mike Olsen

January 1, 2012 after our first Mass together.

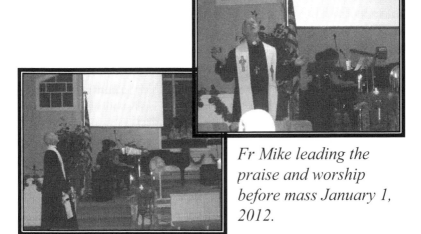

Fr Mike leading the praise and worship before mass January 1, 2012.

SIGNS AND WONDERS

It was not a late night for us December 31, 2011. Mark and I had fallen asleep curled up in bed praying for people's intentions that we had been given throughout the year. At 11:58 pm I awoke with a start! We were just in time to ring in the New Year. I cried, "Turn on the TV! Is it time yet? Kiss me quick!" As we fell back to sleep, we prayed, "God please bless the new year."

The next afternoon, January 1, we drove over to the Crosier's. We were excited to go see the new church. We had a time of fellowship together before embarking on our journey. It was decided that Larry and Mark would drive in Larry's car and Marilynn and I would take my car and drop it off at Mom's in Clarksville. We would pick our car up on the way back home later that evening.

The four of us sat comfortably in Larry and Marilynn's vehicle on the way to Louisville. Larry drove us to St. Columba of Iona Community Church on Bardstown Road. We arrived only a few minutes late. As providence would have it, the mass was not running on time either. They too, were a few minutes late starting themselves.

Father Mike led praise and worship before the mass officially started. He prophesied for the New Year as the Holy Spirit gave him utterance. "This is the year of angels and miracles. The war between good and evil is raging now."

He quoted Jeremiah 33:3, "Call unto me, and I will answer thee, and show thee great and mighty things, which thou knowest not." He went on, "From this rock I will build my church and the gates of hell shall not prevail against it. Dance like a child before the Lord!"

What a beginning!

In my heart I asked to smell the Lord when He would be nearby. Instantly both Mark and I smelled incense.

Father Mike was still before the Lord and gave more utterance. "The joy of the Lord is your strength! Release the joy! Don't be discouraged anymore! The angels are pouring out new wine! There is freedom in this place! Let me bind and heal your wounds. The enemy has no more place here in you. The work is complete. All is forgiven. Now is the time to be blessed! I am calling you to a higher place!"

Marilynn felt he was talking directly to her! God was bringing her from having a wounded spirit to new life! New friends! To a new position where she could rejoice! She felt she was back in the army of God and there was work to do!

As we sang praises, I felt compelled to take pictures in the church. In almost every picture you could see many "angelic orbs".

During the last part of Father Mike's prophesy before starting Mass, Marilynn and I felt these words were for us. "This is the year you break off the power that caused you harm and discouragement! No more! Let go of the words that said you were not worthy or no good!"

Then Father Mike started the mass. From the opening of the mass until after communion, the charismatic liturgy went on as expected. Larry and Marilynn enjoyed the solemnity of the service and felt the closeness of the Holy Spirit in that church.

The homily was about man. It was about man being made just a little lower than the angels. All things are under his feet. We are no longer slaves but children of God. We are heirs. Have the mind of Christ! Empty ourselves! Be obedient! Father Mike started with the gospel of Luke, and moved on to the book of Psalms: How majestic is the name of God! See God as big as He is! His name is above all names! Call upon Jesus! Remember to plead the blood of Jesus over all of your circumstances. His name is above doubt or fear. Jesus comes for His own and you are seated with Him in Glory.

There is a whole other realm that the church does not address much, the supernatural realm of angels and miracles. God is here. He is above our circumstances. He is in the glory realm. Call on angels to bring you help! Plant seeds in others. With praise on our lips, we will see the manifestation of God! Praise silences your foes and enemies! Praise the Lord and watch all your enemies leave! Have a biblical imagination! See miracles all around you! Be like Jesus! Go do the work of the gospel. Consider what God can do. God wants us to believe from small to large. Remind God of what He has said to us in His scriptures. When we make our God big, anything is possible. Then all our problems become small.

After Communion, Father Mike came forward to the front of the altar. He called out, "Someone here has back pain. Come forward to be healed."

I knew this was Marilynn's time for a full healing! I whispered, "Go! He is talking to you!"

Mark in high praise at St. Columba January 1, 2012.

Notice the large white angelic orb!

As she walked up to the altar, Father told this story: "The oil vial I have in my hands was miraculously translated into the home of another pastor who gave it to me. The vial has a little slip of paper stating where it's from taped to it. It is miraculous oil sent to us from God."

Wow!

He anointed each person with oil from this vial. Father started to pray over Marilynn. Mark stood in back of her in case she needed to be caught. I stood beside her. Mike told Marilynn he saw angels all around and in her home. He had no way of knowing there were angel statues all over their house! As he prayed, her back healed instantly and she was slain in the spirit. Father Mike cried out, "God calls you daughter with a purpose for intercessory prayer!"

The next one up was Larry. He called Larry a rock. That he should keep paper beside the bed because he was going to see angels and have angelic visitations. "Write down what you see." Larry too, was slain in the spirit.

Father Mike then went to the other side of the church for more healing prayers. Mark got in line over there. After a few minutes it was his turn. It was as if he could read Mark's mind. Father Mike stated, "God has heard you. He is answering the prayers you have had in your heart right now. I see good, very good things for you. I see a new path."

With Father Mike's eyes closed standing in front of Mark, he stretched out his right arm and pointed directly at me and said, "I see radio and television interviews for you. It is all good."

Father anointed several other people and then walked back to our side of the church. He prayed over more people. I stood ready to catch anyone that would need it. When he finished with everyone else in line Father turned and looked at me. He said, "Well I might as well tell you too." I stood before him both hands raised to receive what he had to say.

Father Mike looked up to somewhere the natural eye couldn't see. He spoke, "I see angels on Jacob's ladder. You have God's ear this year, 2012. God has heard your cry. I see you with a wreath on your head as a crown. You are running the race. Keep running the race! You are just getting started! You have arrived at your destiny, your purpose in life! You will smell the angels, the very aroma of God! The throne room! You will smell the rose of Sharon, roses and flowers. I see your boys walking closer with the Lord this year. God is opening doors for you both that no man can close! He will show your path clearly! Be filled with joy!"

Again, Mark worshipping at St Columba January 1, 2012.

There are at least two angelic orbs above his head!

Fr. Mike then prepared and gave the final blessing to close the mass.

The women all went to the kitchen to prepare the meal. The men helped take down the New Year's decorations. Father blessed the meal and we all went into fellowship.

It was then that the other parishioners came forward and said they had been watching us during mass. They knew we had Catholic backgrounds because we knew all the right responses to prayers. Our backgrounds had told on us!

All four of us helped clean up at the end of the evening. We walked out with the other parishioners taking items out to their cars for them. We were just closing Larry's trunk when I heard Father Mike calling my name and running out of St. Iona to catch us!

"Deborah! Deborah!"

"Yes, Father Mike! I'm here! What is it?"

193

"God has spoken to me!"

"Oh my! What did our Lord have to say?" I stood breathless waiting for his answer.

He said to me, "God said to give this miraculous oil vial to you."

I heard immediately in my spirit, "**Now it begins**." My knees swayed beneath me. Voice would not come out of my mouth. I ran back to the car finally crying out, "Thank you! Thank you!" We all jumped up and down as we got in the car to head back to Mom's. All I could think of in my head was "don't drop it, don't break it, and don't blow it. REALLY don't blow it!"

We hadn't gotten four miles down the road when I noticed the little vial that wasn't two-thirds full had miraculously filled up and was over flowing out onto my hands! God, through this vial was anointing my hands for His work!

I shouted out to the rest of my friends in the car and told them what was happening! They could see the oil coming out of a tightly closed vial, now full to over flowing.

Immediately I knew what to do. I anointed Marilynn with oil and prayer for her ministry of intercessory prayer. Then I anointed my husband for a healing ministry. I did not anoint the driver, Larry in case he would be slain in the spirit!

Our spirits were as high as kites by the time we arrived back at Mom's. We knew when we dropped off our car earlier that she was sick with the flu. We knew what we had to do as we went into the living room. I asked if we could pray over her.

She said, "Yes, of course."

With hands still covered in oil, we laid hands on her and prayed for her to be healed.

At the end of the prayer I did not realize that I was still under the anointing. I said to her, "Awe Mom, when we leave you are going to cough up all this goop and be just fine." Everyone laughed.

When we left, Mom coughed up all the infection. She was immediately hungry and had to eat before going to bed.

The next day she called Sandy, her daughter and told her, "I've had a miracle! I've had a miracle!"

Over the next several days, utilizing the anointing oil, we saw physical manifestations of miracles over and over. Healings from surgeries, averting of disasters, words of knowledge, prophesies, etc...

By the third day of the New Year I was told in the spirit I would be writing a third book, right along side book number two. It would be called "2012 The Miraculous Year". So be it.

CONFIRMATION

By the fifth day of the New Year, I called Pastor Ivie to tell her of these events. I knew that she knew a lot about miracles. When I called her she was back in the hospital with dehydration. Ivie was in a battle. I already knew this was the year of the battle. I told her everything that had happened over the last week.

Ivie confirmed every word and backed it up with prophesy she had been given ten years ago with scripture.

I told her to get well quick. I could already see we were going to have a lot to do.

But fear not, the battle is already won!

SECTION SEVEN
EVERYDAY MINISTERS
AND VISIONARIES

"THE REST OF US!"

*And Jesus came and spake unto them
saying, "All power is given unto me
in heaven and in earth.
Go ye, therefore,
and teach all nations,
baptizing them in the name of the Father,
and of the Son, and of the Holy Ghost:
teaching them to observe all things
whatsoever I have commanded you:
Lo. I am with you always,
even unto the end of the world.
Amen."*

MATTHEW 28: 18-20

CHRIS LUKEN, YOUTH MINISTER
CHURCH OF THE EPIPHANY

Youth Minister: Church of the Epiphany
           Catholic Church for 3 years
College: Bellarmine College in Louisville, KY.
           Bachelor's in Theology
Graduate School: St. Meinrad's 2009
           Master's in Theology
Happily married for two years as of this writing.

Stories come to me from many directions. For example, my friend Vicki has a friend named Gene. Now Gene happens to be a transplant patient who gets to sit on the parade float every year in Louisville, and that is how he happened to meet a young man named Chris, whose job just happened to be helping the people on the floats. Well, he walked up to Gene and they talked. It occurred to Gene to mention my first book that I wrote about miracles, *"Miraculous Interventions."* "Miracles, huh," the young man said. He asked, "Do you think she would like to know about my miracle when an angel came and saved me?" Gene brightened up and said, "Why sure! She is in the process of writing another book right now!" Chris gave a small little note with his name and phone number to Gene, who in turn gave it to my dear friend Vicki, who gave it to me. Four months later, I called an amazing young man who has had an experience with angels. And, the best part of the conversation was that he allowed me to share it with you!

At 14 years old, as a freshman in high school in northern Kentucky, Chris knew he was called to be a youth minister. So did everyone else who knew him. There was just something special about that Christopher Luken. At the time young Chris was not aware of how his relationship with

God was going to come in handy, real handy.

The year was 2002, Chris was a senior in high school in Northern Kentucky. One evening, he was driving home from his youth group meeting. He was eight miles from his home when he started to feel very dizzy and light headed. Feeling poorly, he happened to look in his rear view mirror and saw a figure sitting in the back of his van.

It looked to him like an eight year old girl dressed in all white. She had straight, shoulder length dark hair, with bangs in the front. Chris thought he could see glasses on her but could not see her face clearly. The angel came closer to him as he blacked out at the steering wheel.

Chris had faint memories of his guardian angel driving the car the last two miles home and carrying him inside his house. His Dad found him on the couch and woke him up. Chris then related the whole story to him.

And now I have related the whole story to you.

MARY AND MITCH SMITH
A MIRACLE OVER THE WIRE

This is word for word an e-mail my editor sent me while writing this book. It has been re-written with her permission.

Hi Deb!

This is not a miracle associated with MI*, but it is a miracle! Mitch's on-line friend, Julie, Sunday evening asked him to pray for her mother who was going to have a heart catheterization on Monday because of a blockage they had found in her angiogram. He came downstairs and told me, and we prayed for her to be healed. Since I knew Monday was the feast day of the Assumption of Mary, I also asked Our Lady to take Julie's mom under her care.

Last night, Mitch came in and gave me the report from Julie: The doctors could no longer find any blockage! They found only enough plaque to recommend that she change her diet!

God is sooooo Good!
Love ya!
Mary [Editor]

Love ya right back!
Deb [Author]

"MI" is Miraculous Inerverntions, referring to this book.

GEORGE STODDARD
SECOND CHANCE
(Re-printed with his permission)

Human beings are doubters by nature, and I am no exception. Whenever I heard stories about angels appearing and speaking to someone, I had my doubts. I am now a true believer - a believer who has been blessed with the opportunity of a second chance.

About 2 a.m. on the tenth night following my liver transplant operation as I was lying in my hospital room, I began to see a bright light shining on the wall. I saw what looked to be an angel coming through the wall beside my bed. I could hardly believe my eyes and didn't know what to think. Was I dying? The angel seemed to have no face - just brightness, but she appeared to have a body. She looked at me and said, "George, I am going to give you a second chance in life." I was stunned and completely amazed. After a few minutes the wall shone again, and she was gone the same way she had come.

Several days later the nurses told me about Kara, a 22 year old girl in the room next to mine that had liver problems since she was three. She was number two on the list to receive a liver, but being number two isn't as good as it sounds. Kara needed a small liver, (a child's) which is rare. Needless to say, she was very down in the dumps.

Knowing how she felt, I asked the nurses if they thought it would do her some good if I talked with her. They said they would ask Kara and her mother if they would like for me to come over. They said they would, so my wife and I went for a short visit. I was barely navigable.

I told Kara not to give up and to push as hard as she could, to push for us both, and to pray that my angel would bring her a second chance as she did for me.

201

The next day I was getting ready to go home. Someone had sent me a bouquet of brightly colored, cheerful balloons, and I told my wife that I wanted Kara to have them. When I took them to her she was all smiles, and I received a big hug from her mom.

I told her again not to give up, to push with all her might, and to remember my angel from the wall. I saw the same hope in her eyes as was in mine - the hope that a liver would be available in time.

The next morning when I got home the phone rang. It was a nurse at the hospital. When I heard her voice I was scared because I thought she was calling with bad news about my blood test results. Instead, she said Kara and her mother asked that she call to tell me that my angel had come from the balloons and had spoken to her!

The hospital received two livers that day, and Kara got one of them! She's doing as great as I am and is now back in college with a bright future ahead.

The angel's visit changed my life drastically. I feel better about everything and see the world through new eyes. I have made and continue to make positive changes in my life. I am a walking miracle.

I hope to serve as a messenger as the angel was for me. She delivered a message of hope. Hundreds of people are waiting for organs. By signing your organ donor card you can deliver hope to someone like Kara and myself who are waiting and hoping for that second chance. How many angels are there?

One – who transforms our lives is plenty.

G.L. Stoddard

Author's note: It has been 11 years since his operation and he is now 63. The more George has talked about God and angels, the more the devil has tried to stop him. George has had two massive heart attacks. One was in 2006 and one was in 2008. And in November of 2010 a four wheeler turned over on top of him.

He has survived every such incidence.
How   many   angels   are   there?

As many as God cares to send!
And they can help us in or outside of a hospital!

Bless God!

Kara, in this story, lived another three years until she had a stroke at 25 and passed away in Florida.

But the story continues on . . .
Kara donated her liver to a 42 year old man in Florida. It is now a third person organ.

Remarkable!
Or just maybe, it's miraculous.

I'd say miraculous.

FRANCES GREGORY
A DIAMOND IN A COOKIE BOX

I was sitting at my desk writing one lovely fall afternoon when I received a phone call. I heard the voice of an elderly lady on the other end of the line, and it was not my mother. She started the conversation with, "Are you the lady who wrote the book in the paper?"

"Well yes, I guess I am. May I help you?" I queried.

She introduced herself as Frances Gregory, an 82 year old lady from Laconia, Indiana. Mrs. Gregory also wanted me to know that she practiced the Catholic faith.

My reply was genuine, "It's very nice to meet you. I thank you for calling but, how did you get my phone number?" I could hear her smile over the phone as she said, "I looked you up in the phone book! I have some stories I want to tell you. I think I have some of the same gifts you have. Do you have time to listen?"

"You bet." I scrambled for a pad of paper that wasn't being used for someone else's stories. I put on my listening ears and said, "I'm ready to write when you are ready to start."

Seven years ago Frances' husband, Norman Paul Gregory had to have a lung removed. It was cancer. After five days home he started losing fluid. Concerned, the family took him back to the doctor. His physician examined him and said it was nothing harmful. Norman was just draining accumulated fluid. While still in the office, their son, Mark asked the doctor to take a look at Frances' face. She had three suspicious growths that concerned him. The doctor confirmed that it was a high probability of cancer and she should be seen by an oncologist right away. Frances would have none of it. She was very busy taking care of her husband and would tend to herself later.

Years went by. One of the growths grew as big as a pencil eraser. During that time Frances sent money to the Sisters of St. Bernadette for a new roof. The good sisters sent her back an article about Mother Theodore Guerin. Mother Theodore had just been beatified and needed two more recorded miracles to officially be declared a saint. Frances felt in her spirit this was her chance for a healing! Standing in her kitchen, she reached up and put a finger to the growth at the end of her nose and asked in faith for Mother Theodore to intervene for her. She asked in earnest to be her second miracle. Then Frances prayed.

The next morning the growth was indeed smaller. Smaller still until it was entirely gone and disappeared from her face. She called it a miraculous intervention, and I would too.

After her introduction to miracles in a big way, word got out about what had happened. People called her and asked how she had prayed. They too wanted their prayers answered. This was how she replied, "*for the intention and for God to hear her.*" She asked for mercy. It was during that time she started a prayer group.

One of the men Frances prayed for had a surgery and thought he would never talk again. She prayed for him, and not only could he talk but was out playing golf by the end of that same week!

As Frances went on with story after story, I asked her if she had any earlier memories of such occurrences. The answer came back quick. "Yes."

Evidently, 1957, the year before I was born, was an inspiring time in her life. At that time, Frances was 28 years old and her daddy was dying of cancer. She wrapped him up and took him to the hospital emergency room. While they were waiting for a room, the attendants rolled a woman in on a gurney. She was all alone. Frances walked over to her and took her hand and said, "I'll be here for you."

The woman replied, "You are my angel."

It turned out that the woman had been abandoned as an orphan and never married. She just needed someone to reach out and care enough to hold her hand.

Three months later while Frances was at work at the Naval Ordinance in Louisville, Kentucky, she received a call that Paul's grandmother was dying in the hospital. Could she please come right away? Grandmother asked for Frances specifically. She finished her work quickly in only an hour and a half and left. When she arrived at the hospital and they led her to grandmother's room, Frances reached over and held her hand. Grandmother opened her eyes and said, "God sent you to me." Two hours later, Paul's grandmother peacefully passed away.

In 2007 Frances' brother lay dying in a hospital. His time had neared the end. Family was all around him, and she sat next to him. Frances began to tell stories. She had a dream the night before. She dreamt that she looked up and saw her daddy and two brothers that had passed away. They were all smiling standing on a brick pavement. She asked them, "What are you all doing here?" Her father answered her, "We have come by to get Buddy." He died a couple of days later.

After that, she had a friend who was seriously ill in Kentucky. She had Cancer in both breasts. Her friend called Frances and asked, "I'm not Catholic, but can I come and pray with your group?"

"Yes."

Frances asked God to listen to her friend and for her intention.

The day of her scheduled surgery her friend called Frances yelling, "They did a last minute x-ray before surgery! There is no cancer! The doctors can't find it anywhere!"

Bits and pieces of people's lives unfolded before me on paper as Frances drew the conversation to a close. I thanked her for being brave enough to call a complete stranger and share such marvelous stories. I would personally make sure her stories made it to the next book.

That evening Mark came home from work, and I shared my interesting day with him. Over dinner I said, "Honey, a lovely lady called me today out of the blue. She shared wonderful stories with me. Evidently my book was in the paper."

Mark asked her name, and I told him. He smiled as he replied, "That's my cookie box lady."

"What?"

"Yeah, she lost her diamond out of her ring in her cookie box. That's how I met her."

Of course!

JEAN CROOK
AN AFTERNOON WITH MISS JEAN

I had the privilege of knowing John and Jean for almost 20 years when she felt comfortable enough to tell me these two stories. The Crooks own a costume shop in New Albany. She had helped our family to get together some costumes for our family vacation to Walt Disney World. During the course of trying on this and that, I mentioned I had just published a book about miracles.

"Well, that's interesting," she replied.

I went on, "Yes. I think I am being called to write a second book as well."

"Really?"

"Yes, ma'am. It will be about priests, pastors and other clergy who have miraculous walks."

"Deb," she said, "That is really something. Did I ever tell you that I am an ordained minister? And that I have seen some things too?"

"Oh, really? Want to be in a new book?" I inquired.

She thought very seriously and said, "Yes, I think I'll tell you my story."

Of course, that was the real reason we were there.

Because of the nature of these stories, I am telling them in her own words from her own perspective.
Thanks,
Author

I was a twin. We were seven month babies that lived. This was my first miracle. I lived, and my brother didn't. He died 24 hours after birth. I always wished it had been me that left instead of my brother because I had such a hard life.

They called me the miracle baby. I was the size of a book. I was small enough to be put into a one pound candy box and close the lid. I weighed one pound. I was all wrinkled up and poorly looking. The doctor's told my mother that I wouldn't live either. I was too tiny.

My mother told the doctors she was going to do everything she could to save me. Even though Mom was sick at the time, she would get up, feed me and take care of me the best she could.

There was a lady who lived up the way from us in Alabama. She brought her little girl's doll clothes to dress me in. I had no clothes. I have felt all my life I was put here for a reason, but I can't find it and I'm almost gone.

I responded gently to her comment, "I think you just haven't seen it yet. Or maybe didn't recognize it." I queried, "When did you and John get married?"

We got married on April 17, 1954. Fifty-seven years. We have two girls.

Then I asked her if she owned her shop. "Oh yes of course, us and the bank."

We all three laughed at that. Then she began the real stories I was there to hear . . .

The sister next to me was five years older than me. Her name was Edna Sue. Sue was named after my mother. The strange thing was they didn't get along. Edna lived until 2009 Thanksgiving. She died of an aneurism. She had been living with it for a number of years. But finally it started bleeding out, instead of bursting like most of them do. It took her about a week and a half to die in the hospital. She had hospice offer to come, but there was a mix up. John and I stayed with her all the time. She asked me before she died to please not let her die by herself. I told her, "You won't. I'll be with you." So we did.

What I saw was something a little different to what I've seen before when my mother died. With Edna, it was a Sunday night in November just before Thanksgiving. There was a friend of mine sitting with us for awhile. Well, we were talking when all of a sudden I was watching Edna. I saw a fog come up around her to my right side of her bed. I was facing Charlotte when I saw it. At first, I thought it was smoke. It scared me because I thought something was on fire! I got up and walked over and looked behind the bed. There was no sign of fire. No sign of sparks or anything. I went back and sat down.

I didn't think much about it until I noticed it was going up the wall. Then it got up to the bed. It started up on the other side. It came up and went around her until it formed an arch about this wide. (She motioned with her hands.) It was up to the ceiling. There was some type of movement in it like a working. It stayed like an arch over her. I asked John and Charlotte, "Can't you see this? Look, it's coming all the way around!"

Edna was a very devout Christian. She especially got that way in later years. My mother taught us and read to us from the Bible. We went to church for revivals. As I got older I started going to church with my friends. From then on I went to church too. Oh, it might have been a Methodist, or it might have been something else. I've been to almost all of them. When John and I got married we decided on the Presbyterian Church.

Anyway this grey smoke stayed up there for a short time with me saying, "Can't you see it? Can't you see it?" They could not. All of a sudden it started back down. It came all the way down and disappeared. I looked at Edna and she was gone.

I said that it was her spirit leaving her body. I know nothing about such things, but I just felt that maybe it was her spirit leaving her body.

I inquired, "Do you think it was a family member coming to get her?"

"Well I felt that was what all the movement was about. I really do. After all, Edna had been talking all evening before that. She would try to look at me and say, 'Momma?' I said right back to her, 'Yes, honey. Momma's here.' And I just made her think I was Momma. One time Edna said, 'Helen?' That was our sister that had died last. Well, she finally said to me, 'Jean?' I answered her with, 'Yes, honey. I'm right here beside you.' Of course I was right at her bedside holding onto her, holding her hand and rubbing her arm.

The reason I think this was a miracle is because it was something I had never seen before."

"Well, Miss Jean, it was at the very least, supernatural."

A LONG TIME COMING

Miss Jean and I talked awhile before we got to her next story. I asked, "You're a praying woman. You're a believer in Jesus Christ?"

Jean piped up quick, "Oh, yes! Yes indeed!"

I asked further, "You know you are saved?"

Her reply hurt my heart. She said, "I certainly hope I am."

Then I started preaching. "I know it's up to God to know every man's heart. But, we are assured in that wonderful Bible that those who call upon the name of Jesus and believe with all their whole heart, that He came from God, died for the remission of our sins, rose and was restored to Heaven..."

Jean softly said, "I do."

I went on, "...that we too are saved. When Jesus died, our old man, our sinful nature died. And when Jesus rose, we rose. Our new nature rose with Him. All we have to do is walk right into it. We certainly can't receive it by works. I believe you are saved, or I would not be here right now taking down your testimony." At that she laughed and smiled.

I finished with these thoughts, "I think we will be greatly surprised and blessed when we cross over. The Holy Spirit that God has placed in us cannot die. God is eternal. Our spirit is eternal. Because we have free will, we can choose life! We can choose the one who made us, the one who came to save us. Once redeemed, sin cannot stay in us or condemn us. When we choose God's Son, when we go before God, God sees His Son! He sees us sinless! God then says, "Come back home!" I truly believe you will hear, "Come up hither! Please don't fear."

Jean then relayed another story that I will tell in her own words.

You were talking about miracles. I have another story that I would like to tell you. When my oldest daughter was 13 years old, she was a dancer like my younger daughter. She had beautiful movements when she danced.

One day she came home from dancing class and said her knees were hurting her. She went and laid down. I was taking care of the little one. But she continued to have pain in her knees. Tears would just stream down her face. I knew she was in great pain.

We took her to the doctor that she had seen ever since she was born. He sent her to see a specialist. They did all kinds of tests on her, but they could not figure out what it was. So, we took her to another specialist. This went on for awhile until the time she was ready to go into high school.

At first, she did not get to go in because the doctors were holding her out. I went in and talked to the school about home study programs. The school was very hesitant about it. So her doctor went up to talk to them. He told them, "You are not going to put her into a gym class. When this child says she hurts, she hurts! She will not be coming to school so you work it out! Do whatever you have to do."

We got a system worked out with the phone company to put a box in her classroom that was wired for her to hear what's being said in the class from home. But the teachers did not care to fool with it. They turned the sound box toward the wall or over in a corner.

Well, she couldn't hear what was going on. She'd say to me, "Mother, I can't hear them."

I called the telephone company and told them she couldn't hear what was being said in the classroom. The telephone company told me that they had the line turned up as loud as it would go. They even went up to the school and checked everything out. They told me the teachers have it turned toward the wall. We gave them heck over that.

We told them to turn it toward the teachers so if she had a question she could ask it and receive an answer!

Again, I went up and complained to the principal and anybody else that would listen. They told me the teachers have every right to put the box anywhere they wanted to. Even the doctor went back up to talk to them. It didn't do any good.

Finally, I wrote our representative Lee Hamilton a three page letter on the situation. The same night they received the letter a man from his office called me. He said to me, "Mrs. Crook, I understand you are having trouble with your high school."

I told him yes I was! He said, "I read your letter and Representative Hamilton has read your letter. I am here to take care of this situation. I will go to the high school in the morning. Then I will call you back."

Well, he didn't have to call me back! Everybody at school was calling me!

I laughed and asked, "Is that what you consider your miracle?"

Jean replied, "No, the miracle came later."

"Please go on!"

When he went up there he really shook them up. Of course I thanked Representative Hamilton and this man. By this time Melanie was into her junior year.

The high school wanted to put her in a wheel chair and make her sit by the pool in gym class.

Dr. Adams said, "No! You are not putting this girl in a wheel chair and making her think she is never going to get over this." He told them, "You will send her home early or find a study hall for her."

And they did. But they didn't want to. This is what drove me crazy.

But over time, Melanie started getting better and better, even though they never knew what was wrong with her or what caused it. The doctors called it Juvenile Rheumatoid Arthritis, but in the blood work it was not that. So the last thing that we heard from one of the specialist's was that he thought it had come from an airplane. I know it sounded silly. He thought it was from a virus on an airplane from a foreign country. It did mimic arthritis, but it was not that. This was from a man that was one of the best arthritic doctors in Louisville.

By the time Melanie was getting better, my Mother had gotten very ill. She had kidney failure, and she was in the hospital.

One morning my daughter got up and she walked through the house without crutches or a cane. I looked at her and said, "Melanie? Are you better?"

She replied, "Mother, I don't feel any pain at all."

I said, "Well for Heaven's Sake!" I watched her all day. She walked all day and was fine.

I knew my Mother was dying in the hospital. I went up to see her. I said to her, "Mom, I've got something to tell you and it's a miracle." She asked me what it was. I said, "Mom, you told me all this time Melanie's been sick, you prayed for her to God everyday. You said to Him, 'Please put this on me and take it off of Melanie!' Mom, Melanie is walking today with no pain!"

She said, "Thank you God."

She went into a coma that very minute and never came out of it.

"Wow. God honored her last request."

Miss Jean said, "That was a miracle, wasn't it?"

I replied, "Yes ma'am it was. It sure was."

Glowing, Jean said, "I thought that was quite a miracle."

MITCHELL SMITH
THE MENDING OF MITCH
Four Stories

In all fairness, readers, you need to know that Mitch Smith is my publisher's ex-husband and best friend. But that does not make any of his stories any less interesting!

Mitch is 52 years old as of this writing. I asked him when he thought he came to know the Lord. He had a hard time with that question because he felt he was still coming to know the Lord!

Mitch does not think that miracles are odd. He thinks they happen all the time. In fact, they are so common place we don't even notice them. Except for these following . . .

Mitch Smith surveying our land in Indiana 2012

ST. JOSEPH

When Mitch was in the eighth grade, in 1972, he got sick, real sick. He had Glomerulonephritis. He went into Renal Failure, a bad place to be for an eighth grader. Mitch stated back in 1972, compared to today's medicine, all they had was witchcraft!

The doctors could tell he was really sick. At the time they couldn't do much about it. He was in the hospital and not allowed to move around in his bed or get up. He needed kidney dialysis. Mitch was on the schedule to go down and have the procedure when a little old retired nun popped her head in the door. She visited kids who were in dire straights.

She started to talk to him when she realized Mitch was too sick to respond. She said to him, "Don't worry. Saint Joseph is going to take care of his boy."

That night, Mitch told his nurse he needed to go urinate. They brought him the urinal. Normally he would pass an ounce of urine that looked like a dark cola. It was so concentrated and strong it would burn as it passed through.

But this night, he passed close to a liter of normal urine, without dialysis, thank you!

Every half hour to 45 minutes, his body passed normal urine with no pain. He got very little sleep that first night. He weighed 160 pounds with all the held water, and in two days he was back down to the normal weight of a 13 year old boy.

He still has stretch marks from this event.

DADDY

Later in life, Mitch was diagnosed as infertile. He would not be able to be a daddy. It was a horrible diagnosis, and the tests hurt!

While in the Army, Mitch was assigned as a peace keeper for the Camp David Accords in the Sinai Desert. They were stationed in what is now a booming little resort town. But back then it was just another place in the desert. For R & R, (rest and recuperation), the Army sent them to Mt. St. Katrina's Monastery in Mt. Sinai. They were glad to go because even a Monastery was entertaining compared to a spot in the desert!

Mitch spoke with one of the Greek monks. There were no Catholic chaplains for their task force at that time. The monk asked him if he had any children.

Mitch replied, "No."

"Why not?"

"I can't." He went on to explain what the doctors had told him.

Miracle words came forth from the monk's mouth. "I want you to go over to that well and get a drink of water. I am going to go get you a medal."

Mitch went over to the well and did as he was instructed. Then he walked back over to the monk. The monk was giggling.

Mitch's first thought was, "I'm an American. What's wrong with the water?" There were a lot of the men that were suffering with Dysentery.

The monk replied, "We refuse to drink from that well. Any man who drinks from that well will father twins."

"Oh, really?"

Mitch came home on leave. Mary Dow, his wife did

indeed get pregnant. They went for the sonogram and it was twins!

> *There it is! Glory!*
> *What a miracle to go from infertile to fathering twins.*
>
> *Praise Ye the Lord!!*

Mitch and Mary observing a beautiful sunset out on Mark and Deborah's land. 2012

SECOND CHANCES

The biggest miracle of Mitch's life is something most people won't recognize as a miracle. In his life he had fallen away from the church and from God. Mitch had trashed his life and the lives of his family. He was marking time, waiting to get old and die. Be done with it. He was actually looking forward to it.

One morning Mitch woke up and he knew he was an absolute mess, yet God loved him unconditionally. Even though Mitch was very far from God, God was still very close to him. He felt God wanted him to get out of bed, get dressed and go to the only church where he knew one was. Mitch was just in time for Sunday service to begin. At the time he woke up, he was not even aware it was Sunday!

Mitch confessed he was a drug user, and it went away. He was healed of it. He was then able to make peace with his family, and they were all for it! It is now an entirely different life for him.

If we compared who Mitch was in 2001 with who he is in 2011, you would not think it to be the same person or the same life at all. I reminded Mitch that God gives second chances.

And my dear brother in Christ reminded me that God gives third, fourth, fifth, sixth, seventh chances, etc...

Laughter erupted from both of us!

MITCH'S TESTIMONY
As Real As Rocks

Mitch is a Roman Catholic. He is amazed constantly at the mercy shown him through things other Catholics take for granted, such as the sacrament of reconciliation, the anointing of the sick and mass on Sunday. He stated, "We don't go there to sing songs or hold hands with each other. Jesus is present in the readings. He is present in the ministers. He is present in the sacrament at the altar. He is present in the congregation. He is there four ways from Sunday."

Mitch went on to say, "When you go to a mass that they are using incense, they are marking another way Christ is present in the mass."

Mitch does not belong to a distant God. He belongs to a Lord who is right with us as He promised. Mitch can go see Him on Sunday. He can be in His presence. I commented, "I believe we can see Him everyday. Jesus walks with us."

He made no comment to this as he went on to say that he can receive Jesus in Communion. And when he strays, he can go to Confession. Any priest can absolve him from his sins because the priest is not acting for himself, he is acting in the persona Christi, the body of Christ, God's hands and feet on this earth.

I again commented, "We are called to be the same."

Mitch agreed, "Yes we are! And that is the biggest miracle! That is the one that lets every other miracle in my life happen! We are the body of Christ! The little nun was being Christ for me when she prayed for me. The Greek monk was being Christ for me when he tricked me into drinking the water. For me, it is not a theory or distant, it is as real as rocks!"

221

SECTION EIGHT
DEBORAH AUBREY-PEYRON

"EMISSARY OF YESHUA THE MESSIAH"

Evangelist, Author

BORN: Sept. 30, 1958 under extreme
duress and 11 weeks premature.

FIRST MIRACLE: Three days old.
The saving of my life.

For more on my early life, please see
"Miraculous Interventions."
Home Crafted Artistry and Printing 2012

"Don't grow weary in doing good."

Mark and Deb 2012

ADVERSARY
PART ONE

Back in the winter of 2011 in early January, a dangerous flu was going around. One of the men from our church came down with it, and he came to church to be prayed over. He was running a 101 degree temperature.

Mark and I went over and laid hands on him and prayed for his healing victory. I knew he was in a great battle. Bill had been sick for almost a week. He sat behind us during the service still having trouble with a cough and breathing. I could feel the invading pathogen trying to stir up trouble in our breathing space! I prayed for understanding on how a powerful man of God could get so sick so quickly. That night, understanding came in the form of a dream. In the dream, I was walking out of my bedroom into the living room. I saw small dark figures flying through the house. I knew they were foreign invaders of the dark kind. I started throwing the name of Jesus at them.

"In the name of Jesus," I cried over and over. I cried out, "In the name of Jesus be gone!" They disappeared in a puff of smoke.

There standing at the last, was the figure of a man. He had dark hair and dark eyes. He had on a suit with a black overcoat. He was not ugly in appearance. This world would have called him handsome. But what was in him was ugly. I knew he was my real adversary, God's adversary. I stopped in motion. He turned and looked up at me. I told him to leave in Jesus' name.

He just stood there staring at me.

I knew it meant trouble.

The next morning I awoke and felt poorly. The battle for my life had just begun. By mid-afternoon my temperature climbed higher and higher. I called out for prayer. Our son Andy came over and prayed with Mark for my healing. I felt a little better. My temperature dipped from 102.6 to 101.6 in a matter of minutes. It was to be a short lived victory.

The battle was in full force through the night. I was not used to being sick. I had not been really sick in years. My body ached, the inside of my lungs ached, and I ached all over. Mark took off a couple of days to help me. Over the course of eight weeks, we spent over $800.00 on doctor and medicine bills.

Our pastor's wife couldn't understand why I couldn't beat this. What was my problem? She thought I had "walked farther" than this in my faith. Pastor Fred prayed over me countless times. He told me to stand firm. Do not listen to the flesh!

After more than eight weeks of being ill, I had coughed so long and so hard, the tympanic membrane in my ears had moved causing extreme vertigo to set in. I was filling up a plastic pan with vomit over and over.

Even Mark started to attack me. He said, "What's wrong with you? Why should I have to put up with this?"

The devil was using my own husband against me. I felt like I was losing every battle.

One evening friends came over and prayed with me long into the evening. I vomited up white froth. I felt it was a sign of the attack going on within me. At that time another friend took me to see our pastor again. I asked him simply, "I will win this battle?"

He shook his head yes. Ever so gently he said, "You will win this. Everyday you will get better."

I knew he saw it.

But I was still throwing up. By the third day Mark took me back to the doctor. She gave me medicine to stop the vomiting and coughing so my body could heal and rest. I *badly* needed rest.

Later that day, Mark's intolerance of sick people came to a head in our marriage. Before the medicine could start working, in a plastic pan on the kitchen floor I was sick again. Mark was in the bathroom when I called out for him. Under his breath he made cruel remarks about me. I thought at first I had heard him wrong. I got up off the floor and went to ask him what he said. The expression on his face told all I needed to know.

I went to the bedroom and got my pillow and blanket. I went to stay in the back bedroom and prayed for God's help. There was more than one battle going on, the one for my health and the battle over my husband's seemingly hard heart.

I was exhausted and spent. I had no energy to take on an uncaring husband. I cried out to the Lord, "I'm done! I'm through. Either You put kindness and apology in his heart, or tomorrow morning I'm leaving for my Mother's home!" I was in a state.

After an hour and a half, Mark came to where I was laying down and apologized. He asked me to come to bed. I told him I would but we were talking everything out.

Mark laid down in our bed and put his arms out for me. I sat across the bed. It was time for all the victories to come in. I started the conversation, "Why do you treat me so badly when I am sick? Why won't you help me?"

He replied, "It's not just you, it's anyone. I don't like to be around sick people."

I brought up another point, "I help you when you are sick."

Mark again replied, "I don't ask you to help me. You do it because you want to. I don't want to."

There it was, his lack of compassion for people. A big road block was in the way of his heart, and I with the help of the Holy Spirit, was going to move it! With determination, I set wisdom and understanding in motion. I said, "Listen to me. You want people to think what a good Godly man you are. But you aren't. Inside yourself, you despise sick people. That isn't Christ-like. When sick people came to Jesus, He had compassion on them. He healed them. He took care of them. Jesus is my example for what I do to help people. This is me. This is not you. You are not Christ-like in this, which means you have a spirit on you of an anti-Christ! Do you understand all of this?"

Understanding spread over Mark in an instant. His eyes widened with the new revelation in his spirit. Then he cried. Healing came. Mark apologized to me and to God. The powerful spirit he had on him his whole life came out and left! In an instant, his heart, soul and our marriage healed. Bless God! We held each other tightly.

That very night, the spirit of illness broke over my body. I started to heal.

And bless the man. Mark took off from work to stay with me and help me. He bought me every different kind of popsicle and cracker he could find, Ginger Ale and soup too! He was again the kind and compassionate man I knew he was.

He could now have the heart of Jesus.

We, with God, won three important battles that week. My health, the block in Mark's heart and our happy marriage was back!

The adversary was thrown out!

Alleluia!

THE BEST MADE PLANS OF MICE AND MEN DON'T COMPARE TO THE BEST MADE PLANS OF GOD

The beginning of 2011 went okay, despite my illness, as well as a wintry season could go. But then, our children started to itch, all of them. It started out small. I must confess I was an instigator in this plot, - uh, I mean discussion. It grew on them until I finally had to confront my husband.

One evening after Mark came home from work to his favorite meal and dessert, and he settled down into his easy chair ready for his paper, I started to talk - fast. You know, like when you really want your way and the other person you are talking to is going to need help with some attitude alignment, that kind of fast?

I started the conversation with, "Honey, the boys and I have been thinking about a family vacation. You know, they are big enough now to help pay their own way."

Mark joined the conversation before I could draw my next breath to speak again. He said, "Did you remind the boys we are going to Florida next year with Dave and Dianna Gething?"

I thought fast as I countered, "Yes, but the boys want to go to Walt Disney World this year and not the other studio. And, Miss April has never been to Walt Disney World. Andy knows someone with a condo in Orlando that we can all rent cheap!" I made an excited happy face, held my breath and waited. After all, the first one to speak loses.

So we danced.

He rolled his eyes.

I pouted.

Finally, my exasperated husband said, "Okay! If you can find any way to pay for it, we'll go."

"Whheee!" To me, that was akin to saying, "Sure babe, great idea!" I called all the boys and told them the good news. I started making plans. All systems were a go. I got off the phone with the last boy and said out loud, "Okay Lord, how are we going to pay for this?" It was now in the Lord's hands.

Three days later the phone calls started coming in. "Are you all still doing landscaping jobs?"

"Could you take on this project for us?"

"Is it alright if I refer you to my clients for landscape bids?"

It had been at least four years since we had done any landscaping. It wasn't even on our radar. Another friend offered to make Mark professional business cards. We guessed we were back in the landscaping business.

Within six weeks of asking the Lord for His monetary blessings, we had all our money saved to go on vacation. The kids had to keep up with us!

Early that summer brought the break up of a friendship. The condo we paid for and thought we had a reservation for was no longer available to us. It was money down the drain.

"Oh, Lord, what will we do?" The children cried.

Out of my mouth before I could think I said, "Don't worry children. The Lord has better planned for us than this! You'll see. Just believe." At the time I thought in my head, "What are you saying? This is a disaster!" I had to tell my own self to be quiet and believe God too!

A couple of weeks later was David's 23rd birthday. Mark and I went over to celebrate with him and April. David thought we could talk about the trip and what to do now. We went to their home and had a lovely evening. A home made pizza and Caesar Salad awaited us. Of course chocolate cake and ice-cream was the dessert of choice for the night. We discussed ways of getting around our vacation dilemma. I told David I would work on it the next day. And I did.

The evening of August 2nd I checked the internet looking for a hotel that we had stayed at one other time in Kissimmee. I added up all the separate costs. There seemed to be no way around it. It was going to cost us a considerable amount more.

As I went to sleep that evening, the thought occurred to me that I should check the Disney site in the morning and call to see if there were any specials they had going, just in case.

I awoke the next morning to a call from our youngest son, Andy. He said, "Momma! You need to call Disney this morning and see about reservations. I know David and April would love to stay in Disney. Maybe we could all pitch in to help Ben and Amanda."

I replied, "Okay son. I'll call after I finish my morning devotions."

Are you ready? Read on . . .

That morning at 8:30 am Disney put out the best package deal ever! If you stayed inside the park they would discount your room, your park tickets and each person would get a free meal package! Come celebrate with Disney! And the longer you stayed the more you saved! Yes! Yes! Yes!

The best vacation we could imagine, almost ruined, and now was better than anything we had hoped for! We were now staying in a beautiful resort hotel with all the Disney amenities with a nearly free upgraded meal package, park tickets, etc, etc. There was only one problem. We had to change our vacation by one week. I called all six people and left messages. Then I waited. One by one the calls came in

230

with shouts of joy in each voice! Yes! Everyone was able to change their vacation dates to the end of October. Alleluia!

How is this a God-incidence you ask? Two people from the same family got a word to call on the very morning that an incredible vacation offer came down the pipes. Our cost was cut in half and our vacation wasn't.
Glory!!

SAINT TERESA OF CALCUTTA
PART ONE

The year of the hottest spring and summer on record (2010) in Kentuckiana went into the wettest spring on record **ever**! The mighty Ohio River and all its tributaries overflowed their banks. The even mightier Mississippi River flooded whole towns and regions all the way until it emptied into the Gulf of Mexico.

Gardens had to be replanted over and over again as seeds and saplings drowned in the mix. April saw more tornadoes, over 860 with damage coming out of the west and south that broke records of deadliest and most destructive as well. The season of spring was off to a rough start.

It was the middle of May 2011 when our garden finally took hold. By the end of May, my first book, "Walking in the Supernatural" was ready to print the first 200 copies. (Reprinted in 2012 under the new title "Miraculous Interventions.") Why 200 copies? It was all the money this "mom and mom" organization could come up with at the time.

Our dear friend Kelly had also agreed to come on board as illustrator for the new children's book, "Christmas Chaos." And our landscaping business had taken off like a shot! (I guess no one else wanted to "play in the mud.") We were blessed in all that our hands touched!

Bless God!

Why, even in our sleep we were being blessed - in our dreams, in my dreams.

And it went like this...

I dreamed I was going to meet a visionary. It was not a long journey, but it had its own tribulations associated with the drive. I stopped at a moderate looking brick home. It was a busy place, a work in progress. From children to teenagers and adults, they all had jobs to do. I walked up to the front door, and they ushered me into a small office to wait for her. There was a desk and several chairs sitting around the room. Books lined open faced wooden cabinets along the walls. I did not know the name of this visionary at the time, or what to expect.

She walked into the room still giving orders and recommendations to the people following around after her. She then turned her attention toward me with a big smile.

Her big smile was the only thing big on her! She looked to be about four feet and change tall. And the only way she weighed 100 pounds is if someone put rocks in her pockets!

She started the conversation with great news. She said, "Our Heavenly Mother is very pleased with the book you have written for her Son."

Well, if the dream had stopped right there I'd still be on cloud nine!

But it went on.

How could I explain this to you? The air in the room became "soft", almost palpable with a sweet floral fragrance to it. The visionary was now smiling at someone I couldn't see with my eyes. I was caught up in this heavenly visitation.

She spoke again, "What do you want of us?"

I was stunned to silence. I was being visited by this heavenly host and asked what I would like. They were pleased with my work! I stammered, "Want something? I, I, I want something?" My brain failed me and went to mustard!

Quick! Think!

233

I was so blessed in the moment I couldn't order my own thoughts!

"Uh, I want all my sons to know Jesus Christ! But I also want a home on our land! No wait!! I want the books to do really well! Then, we can put a home on our land!"

I panicked. I couldn't make up my mind. Could I make a list?

The Visionary looked up to Heaven, shrugged her shoulders with a question on her face. Then she turned to me and said, "I will come back and ask you again."

The scene faded away and I awoke.

I still await her return.

SAINT TERESA OF CALCUTTA
PART TWO

I immediately woke up and told my husband of the dream and how amazing it was. Mark asked me who the visionary was. At the time I had no idea. Two days later, at the start of the day, I was in the middle of changing from my pajamas into blue jeans when I looked on top of my dresser. There in front of me, on a ceramic stand was a picture of the likeness of the visionary in my dream. It was the same drawn face, the same petite form. It was Mother Teresa of Calcutta.

Then I had understanding. A Saint from Heaven had come to tell me I was doing good work. Mary, the mother of Jesus was pleased I had written about miracles and given the glory to her Son. I had put their work over what I wanted, which was a job with income that I could help my husband and family, and a home on our land.

And the icing on the cake was they wanted to know what my heart's desire was.

How did I want them to help me?

When she visits again, because she said she would be back, I will be ready with an answer, even if I have to bring a list!

SAINT TERESA OF CALCUTTA
PART THREE

Just a few days later, I was working on some paperwork and needed stamps. My husband stopped by our local post office and brought them home. He did not look at what they had given him. There again, looking up from the stamp was the same face, Mother Teresa of Calcutta.

So I asked for things, starting with wisdom and words of knowledge. I wanted to see fruit from what I was hearing. The first person who crossed my path was a friend of mine who was wondering out loud what to get her husband for Father's Day. Out of my mouth before I could stop it much less think about it came the answer.

Perfect. Great!

There was another person who needed help in prayer over an issue of what to do, again out came the right answer.

Knowledge spoken right out of my mouth.

SAINT TERESA OF CALCUTTA
PART FOUR

With all the wisdom I was receiving for other people, I was still confused about what I wanted to see for myself and my family. What should I have done? As God is merciful, He started sending people my way to help me find the answers.

He sent Kelly to tell me that our boys are already in "saved" status.

Then Pastor Ivie called. I told her everything that had been going on. She prayed and said, "Debbie, why are you asking for things you already have? Your boys are saved. You have wisdom. God has been showing that to you for years. And God has anointed your book! Several pastors have already told you that! It is going to do well. The only thing you don't have that you thought to ask for is a home on your land! For God to finish the work He started there so your ministry can flourish! Don't give up!"

Okay.

Okay!

AN INTERESTING WEEK IN THE SPRING

Did you ever notice how misfortunate events sometimes happen in clusters? Even in the same week? When satan was on the attack, the name of God was still higher and victorious! For example:

   *   Five of us had bad toothaches together.
   * Two marriages came under fire for the exact same reason.
   * My Momma's had swelled with infection and pain over a weekend.
   * Our friend Jim sawed through his hand with an electric saw.

Several of the toothaches got better with prayer, and those that had to go to the dentist, were not nearly as bad as they had thought. All the teeth were saved.

One of the marriages came through just fine and the other is still under construction as of this writing.

I had called my Momma on a Saturday afternoon in June just to talk. She answered the phone in obvious pain. She told me how her hand was swollen and how much she was suffering with it. I told her I would pray for her as soon as we got off the phone. I called my husband at work and asked for him to be in agreeing prayer with me.

I said, "Honey, Momma needs deliverance from this pain and inflammation! I need you to cover us and pray for a healing! We need to agree on this!"

He went into prayer immediately! Mark asked God for His Divine Intervention for Dorothy Aubrey's hand and gave God thanks and glory for it!

That day, she started feeling better. By Monday morning she had a report to give us! Momma called to tell us about her miracle! She even shouted, "Praise God!" Now she believed it could happen to her as well as others, which is the biggest miracle of all! [*Amen!*]

Our friend Jim was working at his home on his land when he and the electrical saw got into a disagreement. That is never a good sign. Blood went everywhere! He had cut deep into the meat of his hand between his forefinger and his thumb. His wife, Lisa packed her husband up to take him to the hospital and called out for prayer. I got a call that went something like this:

"Debbie! I need help! Jim cut his hand through the muscle with an electrical saw. Blood is everywhere. I am on the way to the hospital with him. Please pray!"

"You got it!"

Mark and I started praying for a miracle regeneration of his hand! By the time he was examined at the hospital, the doctors said it was a minor cut.

There was no damage to the surrounding muscle tissue and it only needed five stitches.

What an awesome God we serve!

How many healed people do you know?

ADVERSARY
PART TWO

Spring came and went. Mary and I stayed very busy putting out my first book, *"Miraculous Interventions"*. I delivered books to six different book stores and one physician's office. Over the Fourth of July weekend Arlston's Bookseller's held my first ever book signing. At the time, we broke the record for most books sold by one author in a day. Nice!

During this time, my husband started having real trouble with his skin. His eczema flared. His right knee and ankle swelled and were terribly painful. One night in mid-July, another dream came. The adversary came back. This time the battle went much differently. In this dream, I could see this same man sitting on Mark's health and prosperity– the next battlefields. This time instead of me being afraid and cautious, I went up to him speaking in tongues. Around him and around him I walked speaking the heavenly language. He had no power to interfere with those prayers.

He went into combat. The demon said, "That doesn't mean anything, your speaking gibberish." I kept it up. Now I was smiling. I knew the Holy Spirit of the living God was with me, and I knew the demon knew it too. This time, his face showed doubt. His eyebrows went up. Then it was gone.

Within a few days Mark's skin began to heal. He woke up telling me he felt healing and prosperity coming to our home. As our good friend Mitch Smith had prayed for a home on our land the month before "most rikki tikk." *

*Interpretation: Come quickly, Serpent killer (satan),
    ie: Come quickly and stomp on the devil on your way.

THE KEY

Remember the story about the wettest spring on record? It also ended up being the wettest year on record ever. But in the middle of the downpours, the summer months had all the markings of a drought. First you couldn't plant because the soil was saturated. Then within weeks, it was so dry nothing could grow, unless you knew the key.

Our Mother's Day was spent at McCoy's Nursery and landscape to help Mark's sister and brother in law with their newly merged business. For two days we worked very long, very hard hours. They paid us in plants. Tomatoes and green peppers, oh boy! After we came home I worked up the garden soil and got it ready for the new plants. Within a few days I had all our little plants in their new homes. Now, if it would just rain.

I went out every morning and evening and spoke life to all the plants and flowers we had coming up in the dry heat. I sang praise songs to them. I spoke scripture verses to them. I smiled at them and blessed them each one.

As the last of June moved into early July, we had lots of fresh vegetables ready to be picked. We spread the wealth to family and friends. We were asked over and over how did we get our vegetables to grow large so fast? The weather had been so uncooperative most people couldn't get anything to grow!

I told them that all you needed was the right key to see fruit. God's key.

A CRY OUT

The summer of 2011 was a time of change for our oldest son, Benjamin. He transitioned from a full time job working for a large company to a part time position at the YMCA. This was his own choice. He has a big heart for people and is a natural born helper. His sunny disposition and ready smile attract people to him. It also doesn't hurt that he is tall, dark and handsome.

It was late July, one evening after looking at his finances and watching his savings dwindle down to nothing, that he cried out to the Lord. In his heart he said, "Lord, I just barely have enough money to make rent for August. What am I going to do? I'll go out the next time I'm off and put out applications, but I want to be somewhere that makes my heart happy, somewhere I can help people. Please bring that to me soon. I'll do my part if you will do your part." He ended the prayer in thanksgiving.

The next day was a work day at the Y. Ben was his usual friendly, helpful self. Well, along came a new couple. They had joined up an hour ago. Could he please help them get acquainted with all the equipment and where to get started?

"Why sure!"

In the course of his training them on different pieces of equipment, the wife talked with Ben, and they all shared stories. Then she asked him if he could cook. Puzzled, he answered, "Yes, I can cook."

"Do you like to cook?"

Again, "Yes, I like to cook."

The wife looked at her husband and continued talking, "Would you consider coming to work for our doctor's hospital? We sure could use help in the kitchen."

Elated he answered, "Why yes I would!"

Now they were all excited! She said, "With your sunny disposition you would be a wonderful help to our patients!"

"Thank you!"

Within 24 hours of Ben's prayer, God dropped his heart's desire in his lap!

Of course all his interviews went well. And they welcomed him to the staff with open arms.

Congratulations, son.

Thank you, God Almighty!

HAPPY FATHER'S DAY

Have you ever felt that you really knew someone, all their ins and outs, just to find out that they were a little more complicated than you thought?

Father's Day 2011 was celebrated for three days in our home, much to the delight of my husband Mark. As everything settled down on the evening of the third day and the two of us were sitting in the living room, I watched Mark open his card with lottery tickets and scratch offs inside.

I bent my head down and closed my eyes. I went into prayer. (I know, I know, it's just a game.) I prayed, "Lord, please let him win something."

I heard back immediately, "**HE WILL NOT BE SATISFIED.**"

Thinking I knew my husband very well I retorted, "Oh yes he will. He will be satisfied!"

I heard even bolder, **"ASK HIM!"**

After all, how could I know Mark better than God his Father? As Mark was checking his numbers and scratch offs, I casually started a conversation. "Dear, if you ever won a lottery, you would be satisfied wouldn't you? I mean you wouldn't keep playing over and over again?" I was hedging my bet. Surely I couldn't be wrong. This couldn't be a problem for him without me knowing about it.

Mark replied, "I probably would still play. After all, haven't you heard about people winning more than once? The Lord can bless you more than one time."

Then the Lord showed me a hook. He would be hooked. I started crying and told Mark the whole conversation that had gone on. I told him he needed to go before the Lord.

Check his heart.

And mine.

And yours.

DO NOT FEAR!

Mark and I spent a wonderful afternoon and evening with my mother, Fran Aubrey for her 83rd birthday. We sat and visited on a very warm and humid late August day before taking her out to dinner. Mark drove us to one of her favorite local restaurants. She laughed, talked and remembered about days gone by. At 83, her mind was still sharp, and she can still out clean me!

After dinner, we went back to her home. We sat and watched the local news as she cut us pieces of her birthday cake. She sat down and opened her card.

After awhile we went from the television room to the living room to finish our conversations. Momma asked how the sale of my first book was going. I caught her up to date. Then she asked me if I had made any money off of it yet. Sadly I had to tell her no, not then. We were holding funds out to pay for the children's Christmas book in November.

As the evening drew to a close and Momma got sleepy, we all kissed good-bye and headed back home. We arrived home one hour later, put on our pajamas and watched the weather station to see how the coast was faring against Hurricane Irene. Prayers went up for all in its path.

The night gave way to the wee hours of the morning. I dreamed that I was working for a king. My begging him for help was interfering with what he wanted me to do. He got mad, really mad. Because of my crying out for help all the time, he let people in to take advantage of me. My lack of faith had made him mad, and he was not going to help me. At the end of the dream, I was crying on the floor.

When I woke up, I started crying. I woke Mark and told him God was mad at me! I was sure of it. As hard as he tried to convince me it was a nightmare, I couldn't shake it. I fell asleep in a fitful state. But God had mercy on me.

Between 6 am and 7 am, a revelation came. God was not mad at me for crying out to Him for help. That was my biggest fear coming through. Who is the father of fear and what did that make that dream? An attack! It was an attack! Once I realized that, it felt like a door opened in my mind, heart and spirit. That was when I heard from my head to my ears, "Do not fear! Do not fear!" I knew immediately I had to stand in faith. There was nothing to fear.

Now that I had done all I could do for myself by obeying God and writing His books, helping others out as best I could, now was the time to stand and wait.

Psalm 46:10, "Be still and know that I am God."

See where and what He will lead me to. Then I will see the fruit of my labor of 52 years.

The next morning I woke up with Proverbs 8:21, "That I may cause those that love me to inherit substance; and I will fill their treasurers (wealth).

NO MIRACLE TODAY

Our Walt Disney World family vacation was fantastic. It had been four very long years since our family had all done something that major together. We rented a twelve passenger van for the eight of us. This was to accommodate luggage and souvenirs and snacks for the way home.

We didn't start on our way home until after 1pm that Friday afternoon, giving one final good by visit to the Downtown Disney shops.

We started on our trek late afternoon through Georgia. That was when the arguing ensued. The children thought we should drive straight through to get back at 9 in the morning.

"No."

"We don't want to travel for two days!"

"No!" I was adamant! "Final answer!"

I countered, "It will be too hard on Mark. It will be too dangerous to travel that far as tired as we all are." The arguing carried on for almost 20 miles.

An hour south of Atlanta on I-75, I was co-piloting for Mark when I saw ahead of us in the median, a huge black plume of smoke and fire.

"What's that? What's that?" I stammered.
We were in the left passing lane and couldn't get over. We were headed right for it!! We passed by seconds after the explosion. The fireball was a huge, black angry flame. Something tragic had just occurred.

From the back seat of the van Andy, an EMT equipped with a jump bag screamed, "Stop the van! Let me out! I'm an EMT! I can help!!"

Mark crossed all six lanes of Atlanta traffic to pull over. Other people stopped to help as well. The first vehicle to pull over with us was a big rig. A Red Cross volunteer and a car full of young women stopped too. Andy and his brother

247

Ben sprinted across all six lanes.

The tractor trailer driver who stopped with us saw it all. He related this story: "The SUV was pulling a trailer with a golf cart on it. Evidently a back tire blew propelling their vehicle straight into a concrete support for the overpass."

The driver's side was obliterated on impact. I heard in the spirit "He's dead." Mark and the truck driver ran over to help. I told David to stay with the van and the girls in case it had to be moved due to more possible explosions. I ran over with the other ladies that had stopped.

Andy heard from a distance off, a woman screaming trapped inside the van. By the time he got close enough to open her door, all cries for help had ceased. She was no where to be seen. An eerie silence rested over the scene.

The truck driver, two of our sons and my husband circled the vehicle over and over trying their best to fight past the flames for a rescue.

The Red Cross volunteer was already on her phone calling out for prayer. The other women who had stopped and myself all held hands and prayed for God's help. When we lifted our heads from prayer, we saw Andy with his jump bag walking slowly towards us. I cried out several times, "Son! Are there any survivors? Where are the survivors?" Head bowed, he shook his head no.

I immediately led the women in a prayer for the people in the van, for their immortal souls to be received into Heaven.

Two of the women overcome with emotion, sank to the ground in tears. I asked in my heart, "Why are we here Lord if we can be of no service?" The answer came within seconds.

One of the young ladies overcome with grief, suddenly could not breathe. She was having an asthma attack! My inhaler was back in the van in my purse! I told her,

"Come with me! I have an inhaler!"

I took off as fast as I could with her trailing behind me. I ran full out to get help. By that time Mark had gone back to the van to report to the rest of the kids. As I got closer to them I started screaming, "Mark! Get my back pack!" He couldn't hear me. I ran screaming, "Back pack! Inhaler! Hurry!"

Mark got my back pack and brought it to me. I dumped it on the ground and looked for the inhaler. I found it quickly and told our son David, "Hurry! Take this to the young lady following behind me! She can't breathe! Hurry! Run!!" Off he took like a shot! We could help save one person that day. David caught up to her with the inhaler.

With my second wind I started running towards them shouting, "Two puffs! You need two puffs!"

Two puffs later she could take a deep breath. Andy checked her for smoke inhalation. Hugs were exchanged as we left to get back on our way. There was nothing else we could do.

We all quietly got back in the van and took off. After a few minutes of gentle sobbing, Andy spoke wisdom to our troop of weary travelers.

He said quietly, "Don't own this. This is not you or your family. We all did what we could do. Don't take this in. We have had a wonderful vacation together. That is the way it should stay."

Within five to ten miles down the road the kids started asking Mark questions.

"How do you feel?"

"Are you tired?"

"Do you need a back rub?"

Without me saying one word to them, they all got on their cell phones and I-phones and looked up directions to the nicest, closest hotel we could find.

No more was said about going home without stopping.

Thank God.

We made it home just fine by five the next evening safe and sound.

Again, thank God.

A GOLD CAR

In the spring of 2011 we sold my little Mitsubishi Eclipse, and paid off as much debt as possible. Mark promised we would get another car for me. We had saved $1,000.00 and figured something would beat nothing. The summer went by, and the used car market was as tight as the job market.

As we were leaving for our fall vacation with all six kids, I told Mark, "We have to find a vehicle when we get back home. I have to be able to deliver the Christmas books." He agreed we would get right on it.

Fifteen days later having arrived back home from the best vacation ever; I was on the computer in earnest looking for a car. Of course, I had talked with the Lord about it.

Finally after several hours of looking, The Lord answered me.

I heard out loud, "**You will get a gold car**."

"Okay."

The next minute I saw it on the computer on a lot on Dixie Highway. I knew it was mine! There was just one problem. It said it was grey. Conversation commenced. I said, "Lord, you said I would get a gold car."

"**Yes**."

"The computer says this one's grey."

"**Who are you going to believe, me or the computer?**"

"If you say it's gold, it's gold."

I called the dealership and told them it was my car, and I was coming to get it with cash that very night.

"Yes ma'am. We will hold it for you."

Mark and I arrived a half hour before they closed. We drove the intended car. Even though the paperwork said the car was grey, I kept saying to myself, "This is a gold car from God." I even told my husband, "You'll see. God said it's gold."

251

We waited on the final paperwork to come after having paid all the taxes and changed to Indiana state tags.

When the title and registration came, I opened it and read on the line the color of the car: gold.

Of course it was. I serve a God who cannot lie!
And after the first rain came, the car sparkled in all its golden glory.

Just like the Lord!

HEALED AND WHOLE

In November before the holidays hit, Momma was having a hard time with her back. She was able to walk less and less distance. I was made aware of the situation from various family members. After various doctors' appointments Momma was told, "There is nothing more we can do for you."

She called to tell me this grim news.

I cried out, "Momma! What a wonderful place to be in! There is nothing man can do for you anymore! Now God can step in and heal you! I'm coming over tomorrow night and praying over you."

Her reply was, "Oh I wish you would."

The next day I had some errands to run in Louisville, and then I went over to my mother's. She greeted me in obvious pain. "Oh Momma!" My niece and I took her out to dinner at her favorite restaurant. When we got back to her home, we all sat and talked a little while. After a bit, I said, "Momma, are you ready to be prayed over for your healing?"

"Yes I am."

I asked her where her pain was. She showed me. I laid hands on her and went into thanksgiving and praise. Then, Momma, my niece and I asked God to please heal my mother's back. I left saying, "I will look for your good praise report."

Sunday and Monday went by, but I heard nothing. Tuesday I called her. She was not home. That evening Momma called me. I answered the phone, "Where have you been?"

"At work," she said.

"At work?" I asked.

"Yes, Sunday I got up and could walk. I did my dishes, went to church and the grocery for two hours! I felt so

253

good Monday I went back to work. Everyone asked me what happened to me. Debbie, I told them you prayed for me, and God healed me!" Then she said, "Praise the Lord!"

She was healed and whole!

Praise the Lord back at you, Momma!

SAVED ONCE AGAIN

It had been a fantastic Friday for me, typing and cooking, cooking and typing. I called that a productive day. Mark came home after work, and the smell of hearty beef stew met his nostrils. He hadn't realized he was so hungry.

"Mmmmmmm", he smiled as he peeked at me around the corner of the bedroom where I was still busy pounding keys on the computer. Mark asked, "Are we still going Christmas shopping after dinner?"

"Yes honey", I replied as I printed the last typed page of the day. "I hope they're open late tonight. Maybe we can get at least ½ our shopping done."

After seconds of the soup, we cleaned up and headed for the big city of New Albany. We had some serious shopping to do! And what a time we had! Spoken like a true woman. Almost 3 ½ hours and $600.00 zoomed by. This was our first big Christmas in over four years.

Because of a gracious gift of a family friend we were able to pay off almost our entire credit card debt, and we bought a gently used car. We felt like God had remembered us. Blessings became more apparent as what we had hoped for so long, a home on our land, looked more and more possible. We were looking forward to 2012.

Later that evening we prayed ourselves to sleep. At 6 A.M. the urge to get up and pray and not stop came to me again. I prayed the Our Father and the Hail Mary. I prayed from my heart with tears of thanksgiving and hope for our future. I prayed with my eyes closed and did not stop until an hour later.

At 7 am I heard outside my head in the natural world, a crack of thunder so close it made me jump in the bed. With my eyes still closed, in my head, I saw a beautiful blue sky with white clouds that parted. I saw a gold stream fall from the sky.

I was not asleep but seeing in the supernatural.

Yes, the year 2012 looked very good from here.

THE CHRISTMAS STORY LADY
ALL GOD'S PLAN
THE MAKING OF "CHRISTMAS CHAOS!"

How was I ever to know that when angels walked me to the back yard of an estate sale 150 miles from my home, finding an 1863 German print of Heilige Nacht (Holy Night), the Nativity on the bottom of an old abandoned bread rack, that this was just the first leg of a journey that would span almost 17 years.

In 1995 I brought the print home for $35.00, thinking what a nice blessing it was. It was worth much more than the original $100.00 the brothers had asked for at the sale.

And to think I had argued over and over with the Lord as He told me that morning before my walk to "*take money*." I did not think I needed money. I was just going out for my usual morning walk. I did not want to go to any yard sales. I only brought $35.00 with me to get back home on. So out the door I went, penniless.

I arrived to the point where I was accustomed to turning around and heard from a heavenly unseen visitor, "*turn here.*" Argument ensued. Thankfully I lost. I acquiesced, "Okay, you obviously have an agenda. You take control of my feet, and guide me where you want me to go."

Off I went at a hurried pace! That was how I found at the back of the lot at the estate sale the beautiful picture for which the brothers wanted $100.00. This was another argument with God. "I only have $35.00!" By that time I gave in quickly and walked to the front, gathered the owners around and told them my story. I bought it for $35.00. Apparently, they were much better listeners than I was. I wondered at the time why God had set it aside just for me.

I met Mark two years later. Our relationship grew, and in less than two more years we were married and started a new blended family. As we unpacked our own belongings in the new little home Mark had purchased for our family, he found the picture. I related the story of how the picture came to me.

Within a couple of years married, the Holy Spirit prompted several people to come forward and tell us it was time to build a home. They were sure it was to be south of town. Go south west. Okay.

It was on a warm, Sunday afternoon as we drove south of town to look for land, when my husband was led by the spirit down a side road off Heidelberg. I too heard the spirit say, *"For sale by owner"* and *"$18,000.00."* We turned the curve and four houses down was our land. I knew it when I stepped onto the one and a half acre lot.

When the owner told us it was the front of Bethlehem Farms Subdivision, it did not surprise us one bit. Maybe there was a reason for the picture I bought so long ago to be in our lives. Mark had it beautifully framed as a house warming present for me and our brand new home.

Yet almost every time I passed a little side street two doors down from us, I felt an urging voice say, "You'll live back here one day." I thought it strange because I was very happy with our brand new home. In my head I planned to stay there the rest of my life. Well, so much for what I had planned. After all, they don't compare to God's plans. Sometimes, they even get in the way.

A couple of years later in our life, my back broke at the L-5, S-1. In that same home I loved, I was delivered from pain and suffering with a miraculous intervention from God. The doctor called it instantaneous regeneration. Call it what you want, I could walk and sit and stand again. Glory! Yet God chose at the time to not bless us with monetary assistance for the medical bills. We were drowning.

For two more years we struggled financially and the business I had nurtured to help patients with their medication costs, was failing. I had managed to save over 400 patients homes but could not save my own. We sold our beloved home to keep afloat. Our children cried. Partners came in and took over the business. They sold it to another company who promised better for all of us.

That was when we bought the land in back of our old home, a 10 acre lot on Nicholas Drive. We held out hope that we were being rescued. A week later my pay was stopped. I had already worked the year before with no pay. I couldn't do it again. In short order, I resigned. It could not have been worse timing. It was the beginning of the 2008 recession.

We packed "Helige Nacht" away in a box that was unopened for four very long years. In the mean time, we struggled every month just to get by. We tried to understand what had happened. Where had we gone wrong? Had we stopped listening to God? Were we being punished? The beautiful land in Bethlehem Farms on Nicholas Drive that called to our hearts, now felt like a noose around our necks.

We tried a couple of times to sell it but to no avail. It felt like God Himself was sitting on our circumstances. Pastors Schuppert and Dennis told us over and over again to hold on! God was going to show Himself mighty and make something beautiful out of all this. At the time, it was way beyond my understanding

Shortly before my 52nd birthday, God made apparent what He wanted me to do with the rest of my life. He wanted me to know I was not all washed up, and I was not through until He told me I was through! That was when word came down by different friends that I was to write all the miracles I had seen in my life and those around me. There were patients and pastors, family members and perfect strangers who had come up one at a time saying, "I have to tell you a story. Will you remember it for me?"

"Yes, of course I will."

134 stories later, it became my first book "Miraculous Interventions." After it was written, I sent it off to a friend to read for spelling errors.

Deborah hard at work writing
"Miraculous interventions"

I thought my work was through. January 1, 2011 Mark and I were sitting and relaxing in the new little home in Corydon, Indiana we bought instead of building on our land. We did not have the funds to build. The land waited.

All of a sudden a story out of nowhere appeared in my head. A poem dropped in like water! I hollered, "Paper! I need paper!"

Mark jumped up and got me sheets of paper and a pen. I wrote as hard and as fast as I could for almost an hour.

My husband asked as soon as he thought it safe, "What are you doing? What are you writing?"

I laughed and said, "I don't know, but when I am finished I will read it to you." By the end of the story in poem form, "Christmas Chaos!" was born. Well, welcome to the world little story! It felt in my spirit like a "thank you" from Heaven, but why? All the pieces to the puzzle had not been placed together yet.

I put the sweet little poem at the back of my first book not knowing what else to do with it.

In the spring of 2011 my friend Kelly Riddle had come to stay a couple of days with us for a visit. I read her the children's Christmas story, for it had no formal name yet. As she listened intently, wonderful pictures formed in her mind. She said to me, "Deb, this is meant to be a children's book."

I countered back, "Do you feel like illustrating for another author? And, can I put you on a payment plan?"

"Yes and yes!" Quick answers!

She said she would ask God what to charge me for her services. Within a couple more days, we were in business! Kelly asked me as we got started on our little project what I wanted the cover to look like.

I responded slowly, "You know, ever since I was in my 30's, the same house has been appearing to me on everything I own. A two story brick home is on my coffee cups, my drinking glasses, decanter, even a salt shaker and paper towels! I think we should use its likeness. Do you think that's why these images have been coming to me all this time?" Giggling, she nodded as she began to draw.

Miss Kelly Riddle
Illustrator

I called Mary my editor to tell her about the new project we were starting. I asked her if she would again help me produce another book. Glee squalled over the phone line, "A children's Christmas story with Christ in it! I love it!" I could always count on Mary Bibb Smith.

Kelly drew all the original delightful drawings. Mary colored the picture backgrounds with a computer program.

Deborah and Mary "bringing the illustrations to life", and having way too much fun!

Then, for over four long weeks, she and I meticulously colored each picture with colored pencils to blend them in with the backgrounds. Even my dear husband got in on the act. He drew the back cover, the back of the house itself.

By the fall of 2011 our financial circumstances fell in line well enough that we tried once again to build a home outside of town on our land on Nicholas Drive.

There had been no such thing as coincidence in my whole life. With God's understanding, all fear about starting a new home in our 50's and what it should even look like left us. Everything was being orchestrated for God's exact time.

Glory to God!

The picture of the birth of Jesus Christ in Bethlehem that I purchased 17 years ago, getting the opportunity to buy land on Nicholas Drive in Bethlehem Farms Subdivision almost five years ago, all the pretty little two story houses on our kitchen ware that had been coming to us from various sources, and last but not least, the story that dropped in my head on January 1, 2011, all seemed to point to the same thing.

One day, I may be forever known as the writer of "Christmas Chaos!," the Christmas Story lady who lives on a small farm in Bethlehem Farms Subdivision on Nicholas Drive.

God willing.

Though the house is not built yet, the decision to build is not up to us anymore. It is where it has been all along, in God's most capable hands. Just where it should be.

LEFT: Deb and Kelly
RIGHT: Kelly and Deb at our first book signing

03/28/2012

Deb and Mark standing on their land on Nicholas
Drive in Bethlehem Farms Spring of 2012

"BELIEVE"

OUR FIRST "CHRISTMAS CHAOS!"

It was down to the wire to get our first children's Christmas book out before Thanksgiving. The proof was sent to me the last week of October while on vacation at Walt Disney World. Of course, that only made it that much more special. Book deliveries and public appearances were on the horizon. I was interviewed on radio stations. I had a book signing at Arlston's Booksellers in Corydon, Indiana. I had book deliveries to five different book stores!

I appeared at church teas, private schools, and Christmas programs. The last week of November until December 23rd, flew by! This was the first year I didn't have time to miss my husband! Mark being a bench jeweler, during the season he usually worked 70 hour weeks. No Christmas widow that year!

For having only one month to have gotten the books sold, they did well. Mary and I were able to receive a good portion of our initial investment back. It made for nice Christmas presents.

"Christmas Chaos!" continued to sell after Christmas. They sold at the stores and out of my home until mid-January.

Thank you Lord!

I heard over and over in my spirit, "Do not begrudge small beginnings."

Arlston's Booksellers in Corydon, Indiana during "Light Up Corydon"

Reading "Christmas Chaos" to the Children

ABOVE TOP: Deb with Gael Pack

CENTER Back: Ben Merk, Amanda Wilder, Mark Peyron, BJ McCoy

FRONT: Jacob McCoy, Gael Pack, McCoy Twins Jackie & Jessie and Deb Peyron

THE LAST STORY OF 2011

During this past year we were blessed by the sale of my book to meet and make some new wonderful friends, Larry and Marilynn Crosier and Father Michael and Patti Olsen. To me, this was blessed individuals who sought out other blessed individuals.

By the end of the year our expectations were high enough and we finally felt secure enough, to apply one last time to build our home on Nicholas Drive. By then we had a good idea of what the home would look like.

We were totally surprised by what happened on January 1st, 2012. This event started a whole series of miraculous events in our lives and everyone else's around us.

But that, my dears, will be a whole new book!
Look for Miraculous Interventions:
2012 The Miraculous Year!
The release is planned for summer: 2013.

"Who shall separate us from the love of Christ? Shall tribulation, or distress, or persecution, or famine, or nakedness, or peril, or sword? Nay, in all these things we are more than conquerors though Him that loved us. For I am persuaded that neither death, or life nor angels, nor principalities, nor powers, nor things present, nor things to come, nor height, nor depth, nor any other creature, shall be able to separate us from the love of God, which is in Christ Jesus Our Lord."
Romans 8:35, 37-39

God Bless and see you then!

Deb Peyron, Author

We welcome you to share your comments and experiences with us like minded believers. These in this book have been written in order to encourage the brethren and inspire the secular world.

To contact us, send your email to:

peyronsinjesus@yahoo.com

or to the publisher at:

HomeCraftedArtistry@yahoo.com

or by U.S. Mail to:

Home Crafted Artistry & Printing
1252 Beechwood Avenue
New Albany, IN 47150

(Mail may be sent to the author in care of the publisher.)

30824092R00162

Made in the USA
Charleston, SC
26 June 2014